THE READER'S DIGEST
GARDEN
PLANNING KIT

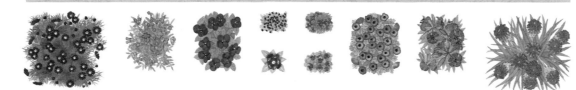

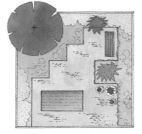

THE READER'S DIGEST
GARDEN
PLANNING KIT

Turn the garden you have into the garden you want

SARAH WOOD

CONSULTANT DEREK FELL

Published by The Reader's Digest Association Limited

LONDON · NEW YORK · SYDNEY · CAPE TOWN · MONTREAL

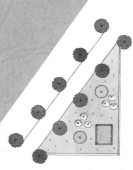

Published in Great Britain by
The Reader's Digest Association Limited
Berkeley Square House
Berkeley Square
London W1X 6AB

Published in Australia in 1996 by
Reader's Digest (Australia) Pty Limited
26-32 Waterloo Street
Surry Hills, NSW 2010

Conceived, edited and designed by
Marshall Editions
170 Piccadilly, London W1V 9DD

EDITOR Anne Yelland
ART EDITOR Katherine Harkness
PICTURE EDITOR Richard Philpott
COPY EDITOR Isabella Raeburn
DTP EDITORS Mary Pickles, Pennie Jelliff
MANAGING EDITOR Lindsay McTeague
EDITORIAL DIRECTOR Sophie Collins
PRODUCTION EDITOR Sorrel Everton
PRODUCTION Janice Storr

A CIP catalogue record for this book is
available from the British Library

ISBN 0 276 42238 4

10 9 8 7 6 5 4 3 2 1

Printed and bound in Italy by
Editoriale Libraria, Trieste
Originated in Singapore by Master Image

Not all plant species or particular cultivars
or varietals may be available in all areas; it is
suggested you ask at your local nursery for
advice specific to your region and growing
conditions. Some species listed may grow
taller in Australia; if this could cause
problems, always check with your local
nursery before purchase.

CONTENTS

INTRODUCTION

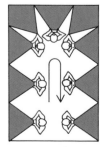

This is a kit to pick up, get excited about and act on. It is intended to make you think about how you feel about gardens, your own in particular. You may disagree with some of the opinions expressed here, which is good. In finding out what you do not like, you will have a clearer idea of what you do, which is the first stage in planning a garden. The design principles can be applied to any size of plot, and once you know what you want, this kit will help you achieve it.

A garden is a magical world apart and when it is well planned and really 'works', it constitutes one of the highest art forms. Only the Japanese have tradi-tionally understood this and their gardens are, justly, admired the world over (and often emulated with less success). Your garden makes one of the most personal statements about you; designing your garden may be the most creative task you ever undertake. If you will get close to what you want, you will make your own paradise.

The kit comprises four major elements. Chapter one, *Garden Styles*, presents eight dif-ferent gardens, each epitomising a different style, even a way of life. Alongside the photographs of each one are pictures of some of the key plants that you might include in this type of garden, while a simple plan shows how you might place the major elements in such a design. Look at the styles and try to decide how you feel about them. The highly cultured, artificial drama of the romantic garden is unlikely to appeal to you if you have ascetic tastes; if you are a modernist the thought of a winding path overhung with dark creepers may make you shudder.

If you like or dislike one or more of the examples, try to work out why. If the minimalist garden only appeals because you would like to live in the

A LESS THAN PROMISING SITE *need not be an obstacle to your dream garden.*

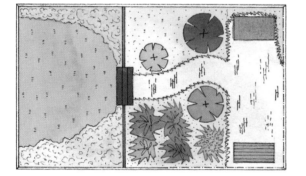

DETAILED PLANS *pinpoint a style's most prominent features.*

COMPREHENSIVE ADVICE *helps you assess what you have and make a scale drawing of your garden.*

CLOSE–UP PHOTOGRAPHS *show plants to consider in relation to style.*

EASY–STAGES GUIDE *to taking a panorama of the garden, a major step in its transformation.*

STRUCTURAL ELEMENTS *are listed and photographed, with advice on choosing and using, taking into account style of garden and practicality.*

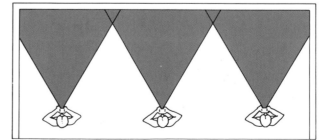

desert, that is not going to help you to design an urban garden that may be carpeted with snow in winter. But if you find it dull and colourless and prefer the instant garden, then you have started to formulate your own garden style, with a preference for plenty of plants and lots of flower colour.

Full of inspirational ideas, chapter two, *Planning the Garden*, contains the information you need to start realising some of your dreams. It starts by detailing the questions to ask yourself and how to assess what is there already, to get an idea of your family's wants and needs. With the 'designer's brief' written, you – the designer – are ready to use the grid, stickers and sheets of surface materials at the back of the kit to plan the garden in detail. Will a paved patio be a useful addition? What can you use to replace an unsightly fence? Do you want a water feature? Read the rest of the chapter for inspiration and for options in paving, soft surfaces, boundaries, pergolas and other landscape elements.

For most people, the fun part of garden design is choosing the plants. Secure in the knowledge that all the hard, or bone-structure, elements are right and sited correctly, you can turn to chapter three, *Planting the Garden*. This shows you how to photograph your garden – the first stage in guiding you through the process of selecting plants – and details the factors to consider when making your choice. Colour, style, shape, mood and texture all play an important part in creating a garden that is personal, as does selecting the right plant for the right situation – to site next to a pond, to attract bees or butterflies, to fill an unsightly gap or to break up an expanse of gravel. Finally, chapter four, the *Plant Directory*, organised by colour and with cultivation requirements highlighted with easy-to-follow symbols, helps you decide exactly what will meet your needs.

Garden design is not a precise art with fixed rules and definite rights and wrongs. It is about finding what is right for you and your way of life and what you find pleasing within financial and time constraints. *The Reader's Digest Garden Planning Kit* enables you to discern exactly what that is and shows you how to achieve it, so that you can create the garden of your dreams.

MORE THAN 200 STICKERS
of trees, shrubs, flowers and other garden essentials.

REUSABLE STICKERS *allow endless permutations to be tried out, without costly mistakes.*

UTILITY ITEMS
visualised, with advice on where to site them.

flowers and green oval aves.

'0cm (12in); spr. 20cm

lgare

·nnual

Scilla siberica 'Atrocoerulea'

lavender flowers and lavender bracts (leaves at the base of the flower head) in summer characterise this open-ground annual. Its leaves are val and aromatic.

'5cm (30in); spr. 30cm

'ritima
·,'

'ıb   for

PLANT DIRECTORY *provides more than 400 plants for every situation and garden style.*

CASE STUDY GARDEN *shows what can be achieved in as little as 18 months.*

INSTANT GARDEN

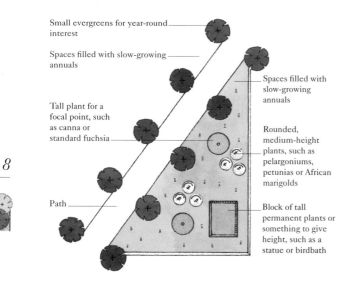

Small evergreens for year-round interest

Spaces filled with slow-growing annuals

Tall plant for a focal point, such as canna or standard fuchsia

Path

Spaces filled with slow-growing annuals

Rounded, medium-height plants, such as pelargoniums, petunias or African marigolds

Block of tall permanent plants or something to give height, such as a statue or birdbath

PLANNING AN INSTANT GARDEN

For flower colour all summer long, bedding plants (or annuals) cannot be beaten. They go on and on, and have a more solid effect than almost any other plants. Although there is no reason why you cannot have an instant white or green garden, why not have fun with a riot of colour? And, whatever you decide to do, you can take the risk of experiment because it does not matter if the results are not quite as you expected – they will last only one season.

There are many uses for instant gardens. They are good when you have just moved in somewhere and you want at least something to look at this year. Equally, when you have planted a bed with shrubs and it looks somewhat empty, fill the gaps with annuals – next year the permanent planting will have filled out. Instants are also useful if you want to experiment with a particular colour before committing yourself. Front gardens lend themselves to instant borders – reds, yellows and oranges on each side of the front path are very welcoming.

Traditionally, instant gardens were planted to a carefully worked out plan, which caused unsightly gaps if any of the plants failed. It is easier and more reliable to opt for an informal arrangement, massing one colour against another, using odd numbers of plants in roughly triangular patches. An edging of white alyssum or blue lobelia will give it a formal touch, if that is what you want.

AN INSTANT GARDEN *is eye-catching. Here a perfect green lawn is set off by a fanfare of pink and red dahlias and salvias, blue lobelia, yellow African marigolds and white feverfew. Behind the dahlias a* Hypericum *'Hidcote' shrub is about to burst into yellow.*

Instant gardens are summer gardens – most of the annuals sold as winter bedding do not flower until spring.

Hypericum 'Hidcote'

Tagetes 'Gold Coins' Marigold

Convolvulus tricolor

Lobelia 'String of Pearls'

Dahlia 'Bishop of Llandaff'

ROMANTIC GARDEN

Perfect for lovers' trysts, Brahms' love songs, or simply gazing at soulfully through rain-splashed windows – a romantic garden is all of these and more. It might feature green lawns edged with natural grey stone paths, exuberant flowerbeds and enchanted walks beneath pergolas dripping with roses and wisteria.

Broad paths – wide enough for two abreast (at least 1.2m/4ft) – lend an air of spaciousness. A balustrade or balcony, a grand sweep of steps, a formal pond and stone statues can contribute a touch of grandeur. Arches, pergolas, trelliswork screens and white cast-iron or dark painted furniture may complete the picture.

It is difficult to create such a garden in a very small space; in these circumstances, opt instead for a cottage-garden look. If you are determined to be grandly romantic – and it is a splendid style – keep it simple. Decide on one effect, perhaps an arbour with a beautiful seat, or a perfect flowerbed designed around a huge

bush of the old rose 'Roseraie de l'Haÿ' wafting its heavy scent into the house.

Purple, pink, white and blue are easier to incorporate into romantic gardens than bright colours like orange (although Monet used it to great effect at Giverny). Pale or deep and glossy green leaves, like those of camellias (very romantic plants), and white variegated foliage also fit the theme well. Or add sophistication with a combination such as *Artemisia* 'Powis Castle' and *Heuchera* 'Palace Purple'.

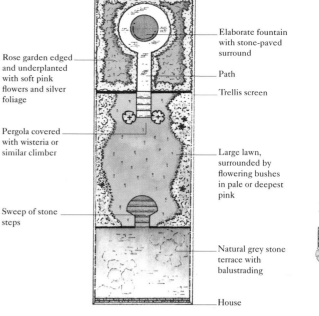

- Elaborate fountain with stone-paved surround
- Rose garden edged and underplanted with soft pink flowers and silver foliage
- Path
- Trellis screen
- Pergola covered with wisteria or similar climber
- Large lawn, surrounded by flowering bushes in pale or deepest pink
- Sweep of stone steps
- Natural grey stone terrace with balustrading
- House

PLANNING A ROMANTIC GARDEN

9

IN A ROMANTIC GARDEN *the air may be perfumed with the scents of honeysuckle and roses – such as 'Reine Victoria'. Here a huge* Philadelphus *'Virginal' stoops over the herb garden, hidden* *behind its trellis screen. Stately delphiniums stand in front. Ideal for twilight assignations on hot summer evenings, the summerhouse is set for an intimate supper for two.*

Paeonia 'Sarah Bernhardt'

Delphinium

Camellia x *williamsii* 'Donation'

Lonicera Honeysuckle

Philadelphus 'Virginal'

Container Garden

Even if you have no land, you can still have a garden. The time-honoured way to do so is to use containers. You can site a container garden on your windowsill or even inside your window, by your front door, in a tiny yard, or on a balcony or flat part of your roof (but you must take the structure into account here; place containers around the edges and if you are in any doubt consult a structural engineer). If you have more space, and you want to sit in it, consider that first. Decide where it is sunny and shady, and provide shelter from the wind. A trellis of slatted bamboo or one covered in climbers will reduce wind and look pretty as well.

Your containers themselves give a strong visual message – they can be plain terracotta, fancy terracotta with flowery motifs, stark white concrete, sensuous curved pithoi or homemade using paint or mosaic on old tins and boxes. The possibilities for siting them are endless, too: place them on staging, steps, brackets on the wall, old sewing machine tables and even in old troughs or sinks.

Plants can be equally varied but, generally, drought lovers are the most likely to flourish, while those that like moist conditions will be unhappy because a container dries out so quickly. Otherwise, your limitations are the size of the plant and the microclimate of your container garden. You can create seasonal effects by swapping pots around, as long as you have somewhere to hide the finished ones; if you want different colours each year, use annuals; fruit and vegetables such as tomatoes and strawberries make decorative – and edible – container plants. But whatever you choose, remember to water your plants – up to twice a day in midsummer – and have them looked after when you are away.

A CONTAINER GARDEN *is bursting with colour and life. The containers here are all terracotta, some with intricate flower or leaf moulding, others with a basketwork effect. Arranged for maximum impact, with smaller ones clustered at the front and larger ones behind, they overflow with flowers and greenery.*

Bergenia 'Pugsley Pink'

Calendula officinalis Pot marigold

Sedum spectabile 'Autumn Joy'

PLANNING A CONTAINER GARDEN

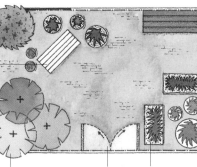

Large fragrant climber, such as a rose, on trellis

Seat surrounded by pots of fragrant flowers

Old steps used as staging for plants

Large tubs, with orange, lemon or olive trees – to be taken indoors for winter

Shady corner, perhaps a 'grove' of small trees, kept well watered

Door

Boxes for vegetables, perhaps tomatoes and lettuce in summer

MYSTERIOUS GARDEN

A quiet place, the mysterious garden is somewhere to walk, look and think, perhaps even to hide. It may have green lawns fringed with leafy beds, white flowers that gleam in the moonlight, paths that meander through deep shade, opening out to calm glades or a sheltered sun-filled corner. Or perhaps your mysterious garden is a beautifully walled stone courtyard with a single bench. This garden is not an 'outdoor room', but somewhere unique to itself.

Every garden needs an element of the mysterious, if only a niche to read undisturbed. Some are wholly defined by it. There is nothing more mysterious than the Ryoan-ji Zen stone garden in Kyoto, Japan, where 15 rocks, arranged in perfect visual balance, convey a sense of infinity.

What do you want to do here? If you want to sit and gaze, with only essentials to aid your contemplation, everything must be perfect – simple paving, a smooth lawn, a wonderful tree. Or do you want an overgrown garden, with shady nooks, mossy ruins and a still dark pool – which can be faintly sinister too. Paths might disappear off in different directions, or tempt you through an archway, or lead you to a stone seat or statue.

Large-leaved green plants, such as *Rheum palmatum* and *Hydrangea sargentiana*, often work well, as do pale or white flowers like arum lilies, with perhaps occasionally a blood red rose.

A MYSTERIOUS GARDEN *is a place for quiet contemplation, a shady corner in which to hide away. The pergola, stained soft blue-grey, is overhung with* Akebi quinata *and planted around with shade lovers such as hostas and ferns. Low clipped box and a large pot of ligularia with red undersides to its leaves give a handsome contrast to the softness of the planting around the pergola. Beneath, ghostly marble statues recall the 18th-century grottoes used by landscape gardeners.*

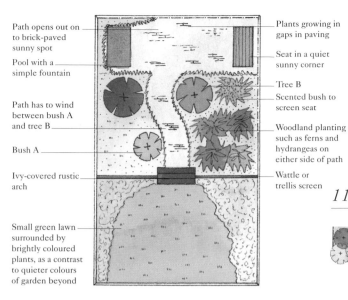

Path opens out on to brick-paved sunny spot

Pool with a simple fountain

Path has to wind between bush A and tree B

Bush A

Ivy-covered rustic arch

Small green lawn surrounded by brightly coloured plants, as a contrast to quieter colours of garden beyond

Plants growing in gaps in paving

Seat in a quiet sunny corner

Tree B

Scented bush to screen seat

Woodland planting such as ferns and hydrangeas on either side of path

Wattle or trellis screen

PLANNING A MYSTERIOUS GARDEN

Polypodium vulgare 'Cornubiense'

Hedera Ivy

Rheum palmatum Ornamental rhubarb

Rhus typhina Staghorn sumach

Aconitum napellus Monkshood

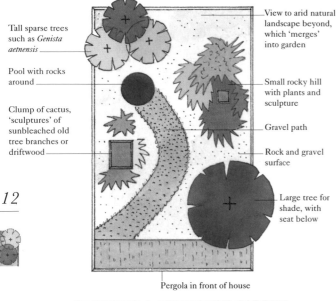

Tall sparse trees such as *Genista aetnensis*

Pool with rocks around

Clump of cactus, 'sculptures' of sunbleached old tree branches or driftwood

View to arid natural landscape beyond, which 'merges' into garden

Small rocky hill with plants and sculpture

Gravel path

Rock and gravel surface

Large tree for shade, with seat below

Pergola in front of house

PLANNING A MINIMALIST GARDEN

MINIMALIST GARDEN

Any garden that consists of a few simple elements, arranged with care – a square of green grass with a green hedge and a white stone path, for example – can be classed as minimalist in effect. Often, however, the most successful minimalist gardens reflect the lines and colours of the natural environment – a pool of blue water echoing the sea in a coastal location, an outcrop of cacti and succulents in the desert or an island of ornamental grasses in a grassland setting.

Creating such gardens requires time spent observing and just feeling the spirit of the place. Imposing your dream may not work. You must consider above all the vital elements of the space.

Is it hot and dry, or moist and misty? Is it windy? Such factors will determine the elements you place in the garden. You can still have the practical things, such as somewhere to sit, a screen or a frame for a view – but always think outward from the characteristics of the place as a whole. If your area is rainy and misty, somewhere to sit will be a shelter where you can enjoy the rain, but you may have to forgo dianthus and lavender – they come from warm, dry climates. Perhaps vibrant green plants, tree ferns and mosses might form the essentials of your garden.

Many of these gardens are made in extreme climates. For years, gardeners in hot places have tried to exert their control over the land, in the process using scarce water to maintain an improbable greenness that almost always jars with the surroundings. The minimalist garden in this climate usually works best when it echoes the desert outside, with local rocks or boulders and naturally adapted plants such as cacti which may, none the less, have originated elsewhere.

A MINIMALIST GARDEN *for a desert landscape must of necessity feature drought-resistant plants like agave, aloes and cacti which are ideally suited to the arid climate. Here elegant cacti grow in the dry sand surrounding a small pool, which reflects the everlasting blue of the sky. The overhanging tile roof provides deep cool shade to contrast with the heat and dryness of the garden.*

Cortaderia selloana

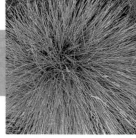

Festuca glauca Blue fescue

Agave

WILDLIFE GARDEN

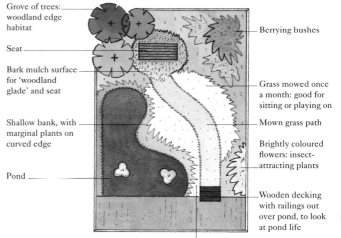

Grove of trees: woodland edge habitat

Seat

Bark mulch surface for 'woodland glade' and seat

Shallow bank, with marginal plants on curved edge

Pond

Berrying bushes

Grass mowed once a month: good for sitting or playing on

Mown grass path

Brightly coloured flowers: insect-attracting plants

Wooden decking with railings out over pond, to look at pond life

Damp meadow plants

PLANNING A WILDLIFE GARDEN

Like a minimalist garden, a wildlife garden evolves from your area's natural landscape. The difference is that here your aim is to encourage the greatest possible diversity of flora and fauna. You will have to decide how purist you want to be. What is important, however, is to develop a clear framework, otherwise your garden will look messy and shapeless. English hedgerows are lovely only because they have a strong shape – the line of the hedge and the land. You must make that shape yourself: clear lines, careful siting of a pond and a good place to sit all make the outline within which your plants can flourish and look attractive.

The nearer the house, the more formal the layout should be, so site the tidy lawn here and leave the meadow to the back of the garden. You can have a good wide path leading up there: no need for a narrow wiggly path just because it is meant to be wild.

Contact your local wildlife association for advice on suitable plants, and on which animals, birds and insects you can hope to attract. Species' needs vary, but many birds prefer bushy or thorny shrubs which offer protection from predators for their eggs and young. Insects and some birds can be highly plant specific in their choice of food,

others are less so. And although grains, fruits and berries are essential to attract birds, do not overlook the importance of water. If there is no stream or pond in your garden, consider installing rigid liners to create drinking pools and using a hidden pump to provide a constant source of running water. Perhaps nothing is quite so musical as the sounds of birdsong and frogs mingling with the splashing of water.

A WILDLIFE GARDEN must have a place to sit and a view to be enjoyed to the full. A pond is usually an essential feature, too. Water lilies attract dragonflies and other insects, and their floating leaves provide shelter for frogs and fish. The tall meadow grasses and dense growing bushes give cover for small mammals, and flowering perennials attract butterflies.

Nymphaea Water lily

Helianthus annuus Sunflower

Echinacea purpurea Coneflower

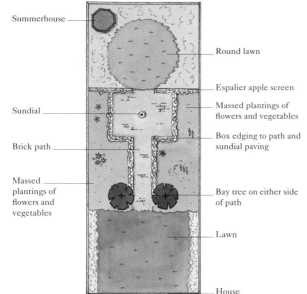

Summerhouse

Round lawn

Espalier apple screen

Sundial

Massed plantings of flowers and vegetables

Brick path

Box edging to path and sundial paving

Massed plantings of flowers and vegetables

Bay tree on either side of path

Lawn

House

PLANNING A COTTAGE GARDEN

COTTAGE GARDEN

One of the most satisfying gardens to possess, the cottage garden allows a little untidiness and a lot of impulsive buying – and everyone loves the effect. To achieve this daydream, you first need a strong framework. The classic cottage-garden path leads to the front door and has flowers spilling in from each side.

Start with straight lines, low clipped box hedges, paths under pergolas leading to sundials, or neat little lawns and cosy places to sit. Make sure that the pergola is high and wide enough for plants to hang down and spread in. If you can obtain them, use old bricks; if not, put down gravel edged with brick, tile or wood edgers, or natural grey stone crazy paving.

Having exercised restraint as far as the outline is concerned, you can be free with the plants. Profuse overplanting, bursting with controlled chaos, is the idea: dahlias, lupins, pinks, snapdragons, red-hot pokers, Canterbury bells, hollyhocks, all the plants that have childhood memories. Add some herbs such as rosemary, parsley, thyme and sage, and if you have an old apple tree, so much the better.

You can have a colour scheme if you like, but it is not necessary. Aim for different colours with lots of white, and include berrying plants like pyracantha and *Cotoneaster* 'Cornubia' with its hanging bunches of berries. The plants may almost totally overwhelm the garden – hence the need for discipline in the first place.

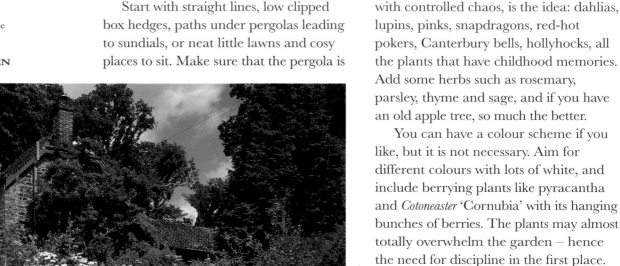

IN A COTTAGE GARDEN, *the path leads up some steps to the front door, hidden behind beds overflowing with colourful flowers – big white Shasta daisies, blue delphiniums, red hollyhocks, orange nasturtiums, pink nicotiana tucked in for the summer, a lavender bush – the list is endless. This is not a garden for sophisticated shapes and colours, so avoid conifers, as well as red and steely blue foliage. Plan carefully so that you have evergreens for the winter.*

Alcea rugosa Hollyhock

Salvia officinalis Sage

Kniphofia Red-hot poker

Achillea 'Coronation Gold'

Petroselinum crispum Parsley

MODERN ARCHITECTURAL GARDEN

Sharing the sparse planting and clean lines of minimalist gardens, those designed in a modern style are often urban, their function simply to provide an aesthetically pleasing space in which to be outside. That is not to say that they do not need planning; in fact, they probably need more thought than other styles. Lacking the minimalist inspiration from nature, modern gardens take the architectural lines and the functional simplicity of the house as their starting points. So awkward curves and elaborate arches draped with romantic plants may be out of place here. Aim to reflect the lines of the house in plants and materials.

There are no rules as to what materials to use, but for practical reasons these tend to be gardens with hard surfaces: paving of concrete, tiles or brick, decking if the climate is dry, and sometimes steel or plastics. Nothing is 'incorrect', as long as it works well.

Plants in such gardens are often sculptural or dramatic. Grasses, in particular, complement the bold lines of buildings, especially the fountain-like forms of miscanthus and stipa. Distinctive shrubs like the crisp-looking *Osmanthus delavayi* or chunky, low-growing *Viburnum davidii* have dark green leaves, but you could also opt for a bright slash of red and choose a line of pelargoniums.

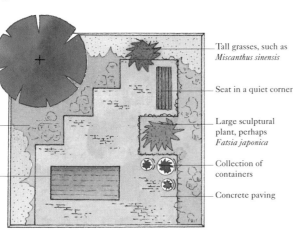

beautiful tree – gleditsia, jacaranda – with plants beneath

gravel to extend paving, with plants growing in gravel

large table for al fresco meals

Tall grasses, such as *Miscanthus sinensis*

Seat in a quiet corner

Large sculptural plant, perhaps *Fatsia japonica*

Collection of containers

Concrete paving

PLANNING A MODERN ARCHITECTURAL GARDEN

IN THIS MODERN GARDEN *a stunning blue slate path leads to the house, itself painted in the same clear blue.*

Large Chinese pots, on slate plinths, flank the path. The camellias which they contain will fill out and give a

strong dark element in the sea of blue. Striking foliage plants such as ferns and bamboos complete the effect.

Verbascum bombyciferum

Achnatherum calamagrostis

Osmanthus delavayi

YOUR WANTS AND NEEDS

You now probably have a broad notion of the style of garden you would like, so it is time to start putting those ideas into practice. To do so, take stock of what you have already. You need to know your garden's measurements, what sort of soil you have and your garden's aspect, in other words the direction from which the sun crosses your garden. All these are elements over which you have little or no control. But you also need to consider how these factors might affect what you want to do in the garden and look at how they fit your family's needs and wishes.

A simple questionnaire is often the easiest way to get an idea of what you really want from your garden. Look at the questions below.

How do you want to use your garden?
Somewhere to sit/somewhere to entertain/a place for the children to play/beautiful views from the house/ to stroll in

Do you intend to work in the garden?
Every day/weekends only/evenings only/not at all
Do you and a partner plan to share chores?

Do you like to barbecue/picnic/dine in the garden?
Yes/No
If yes, do you like to do so in the sun?

Do you want to sit alone in the garden?
Yes/No
If yes, in the sun or shade?

Do you need a compost bin/dustbins/dog kennel/ shed/greenhouse/somewhere to hang washing?
Do you want such items hidden from view?

Would you like any of the following in your garden: lawn/patio/pool/herbs/vegetables/ containers/pergola/barbecue/summerhouse?

How big is your garden? Is it too long? Too short? Too sunny? Too shady? Is it overlooked?

What is your garden's aspect (from which direction does the sun cross the garden)?

What are the main characteristics of the garden's soil (see box right)? What is its main water source?
City mains/well/river/rainfall

BEFORE NEW PLANTS *have had a chance to settle, and after building work, your garden may look raw and new. But it will soon take shape. This garden has been designed around several good plants from the existing garden, including a large bamboo and a dogwood, which will help give it an early feeling of maturity.*

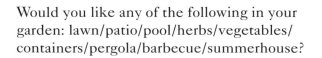

AFTER ONLY 18 MONTHS, *the ground-cover planting is growing profusely and has started to overflow the beds and soften the hard lines of the brick and concrete paving. The dogwood, now in full flower, proves that it was worth keeping.*

The stages described here and on pp. 18–19 show you how to go about planning your own garden. Your situation and responses to the questions may well be different, but you can use the following 'case study' as a model on which to construct your own plan.

You and your partner both work all day and have two children. You have little time for gardening but like to sit out on fine evenings and have friends round at the weekend. The garden is 10m (33ft) long, narrow and gets late afternoon sun.

The most important question for you was the first: how do you want to use the garden? If you want to sit and read, your sitting area will be the first thing to place; if you want something to look at from your living-room window, the picture from there will be your priority.

You decide you want somewhere to sit, eat and entertain, so think about that first.

TESTING YOUR SOIL
There are various types of soil, defined by their basic elements, although they may be more or less mixed with one another and with decayed organic matter. The best way to feed your soil is with compost, made from kitchen and garden vegetable waste.
• *Sandy soil* is easy to dig over unless it also has a lot of stones and gravel. It warms up quickly in spring, but water drains through freely, taking nutrients away. Adding humus and mulching with organic matter will improve its composition and water-retaining ability.
• *Lime or chalky soil* is similar in use to sandy soil, but it is always alkaline.
• *Clay soil* is heavy and sticky to work, but very rich once cultivated. It is slow to warm in spring. Organic matter helps to break it up.
• *Loamy soil* is a mixture of clay and sand, the ideal combination for gardeners.
• You can test for acid or alkaline soil using a simple kit from a garden centre. The kit will include instructions, plus indications of the preferences of many common plants.
• It is easy to add lime to acid soil to make it more alkaline, but difficult to make alkaline soil acid, so grow acid-loving lime-hating plants either in special beds with imported acid soil or in large containers.

FROM IDEAS TO REALITY

YOU WILL NEED

Your garden's measurements
Scissors, pencil and ruler

Grid at the back of
the book

Stickers at the back
of the book

Sheets of surface
materials at the
back of the book

Draw a rough outline of your garden on a piece of scrap paper; then, using your longest tape measure or a piece of string marked off in metres or feet, go out and measure all its dimensions (remember to include all the awkward angles). Write them on to your outline.

Divide the garden into suitable working units. If it is large, each large square on the grid might represent 1.5m (5ft); if small, each small square might represent 30cm (12in). But choose a unit that you can work in comfortably and that allows you to fit either the whole garden or a reasonably self-contained part of it on to the grid.

Using a pencil and ruler, draw in the outline of the garden and the walls of the house. Indicate doors and windows in their correct place, noting doors that open outward, and how far they reach. Show anything that you cannot change or remove.

If you have a lawn and want to keep all or most of it, cut out a sheet of grass to its dimensions and slip it under the acetate. Site and size the patio (see box right). What sort of hard surface do you want? Look at the options on pp. 20–21. Think about the style(s) you liked; consider the pros and cons of the different materials; visit garden centres; look at what your friends have; ask their experience of the materials you may be thinking of using. In this example, you decide to use brick.

• Draw the garden outline and mark windows and doors

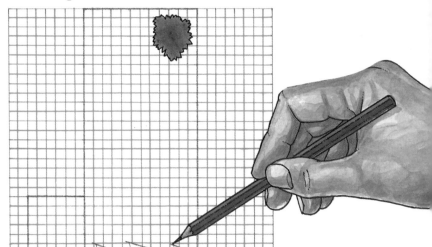

• Cut out an area of paving

• Place paving under the acetate

• Experiment with the stickers

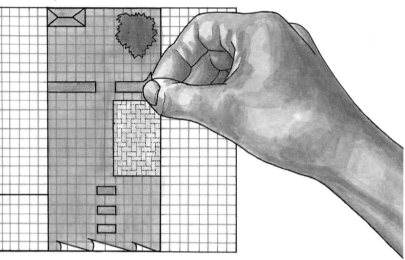

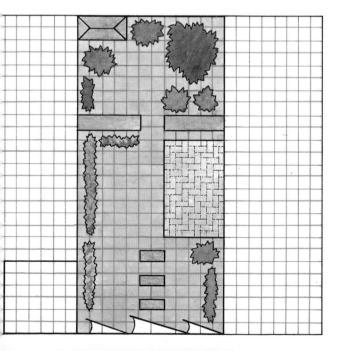

Cut out an area of paving and slip it under the acetate in the right place on the scale drawing of your garden. This is your new patio.

The next stage will be obvious. What are you going to do about the gap between the house and the patio? Do you need a path? (If you are only going to use the patio in summer, stepping stones may be enough.) Try out the effect of some of the round or square stickers to see. You now have the main 'hard' elements of your new garden.

Is the patio a little intrusive? Try enclosing it with a block of plants or some trellis. Using the stickers, try out different combinations. You like the look of the trellis, which is starting to cut off the back of the garden. Play around with this. What about a second piece on the other side of the garden? This starts to screen the bottom of the garden, giving a grassy area for the children to play, which need not be kept so tidy.

Think again about what else you need – barbecue, clothes line, herbs, for example (see Checklist, pp. 32–33) – and use the stickers to help you position all these elements.

By now the shape of your garden should be fairly clear and you can start to put in the blocks of plants. Remember that planting beds are best defined by the shape of the lawn and/or patio, so now you need to make any adjustments to the grass that is there already or, if you are starting afresh, cut out a piece of grass to the shape you want and slip that in place under the acetate. You now have your flowerbeds – in the spaces that are left. Use the different coloured stickers to fill them in.

• **WHERE TO SITE THE PATIO**
If you want to sit in the sun on your new patio, think about what time of day you are most likely to use it, and when your garden is at its sunniest. Choose the spot that gets the right amount of sun at the time you want to sit outdoors, but remember that if you are looking in midsummer, you will get less sun at other times of year.

• **HOW TO SIZE THE PATIO**
The size of the patio is vital if you want to sit and eat there. Do you have a table and chairs for the garden? If not, take the kitchen table and chairs and put them where you want to sit. Leave a margin so that you can move around the table and push chairs out. As a rough guide, allow 1.8 x 1.8m (6 x 6ft) for two people, and 3.5 x 3.5m (12 x 12ft) for six to eight, but your measurements using your furniture will be best.

You now have an idea of the area of your hard surface.

HARD SURFACES

Ideal as a level area for tables and chairs, hard surfaces come into their own in winter when grass may be unsightly and, along with some types of wood, damp or slippery to walk on. Apart from sweeping and removing odd weeds, hard surfaces are largely maintenance free. Of course, stretching out in the sun on an area of paving is not the same as lying on a lawn, nor does it provide such a soft landing for children's games. But the major disadvantage of hard surfaces is cost – most are expensive to buy and can be tricky to lay, which may involve additional expense. So it is extremely important to look carefully at the different types of material before you make your decision.

Hard surfaces often appear harsh unless softened with plants; heat lovers in particular, such as cistus and sage, can look good spreading over paving, and the warmth reflected from the stone brings out their scent. Most people opt for a combination of hard and soft surfaces, but in a small garden, a hard surface can be simpler and more effective.

CHEQUERED TILES *(below) look smart, but need a simple frame. They are costly to buy and to lay, and it is difficult to replace odd broken ones.*

TILES *in different colours (above) can be cheering, but need simple surrounds. Good for paths and small areas; a large expanse can be overpowering.*

CONCRETE SETTS *have similar advantages to bricks in terms of versatility and are more economical than granite setts.*

GRANITE SETTS *are hard-wearing and attractive, but must be laid by a professional. A good alternative to brick in cottage and other informal gardens.*

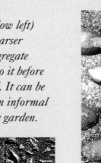

GRAVEL *can be softened with plants and is a cheap option for large areas, but it can be trodden indoors if too close to the house.*

ASPHALT *is strong and hard-wearing and, like concrete, good for large utility areas such as drives. Its appearance can be softened by rolling*

shingle (below left) or, for a coarser texture, aggregate (below) into it before it sets solid. It can be too harsh in informal parts of the garden.

COBBLES SET IN CONCRETE *can be more expensive than cobbles alone and are difficult to walk on. But they look good and are easy to sweep clean.*

MODERN PAVING SLABS *are smart and available in several different shapes and sizes, but they are expensive to lay and tend to be slippery when damp.*

HERITAGE PAVING *is a good artificial substitute for natural stone. Hard-wearing and practical in utility and more informal areas.*

NATURAL STONE PAVING, *available in a variety of shades, wears better than any other surface. Ideal for paths and patios.*

SLATE *comes in many shades from blue-grey to pale grey, which all deepen after rain. Buy thick pieces – thin ones flake with wear and after excess rain.*

BRICKS *(left) are versatile; they can look traditional or modern, be laid in lines or circles and be used with stone, concrete or gravel. Buy bricks suitable for paving – these will withstand frost. Concrete pavers have a similar, but sharper, look.*

HERRINGBONE BRICKS *are perfect for cottage-garden paths, but can be costly since their straight edges must be individually cut.*

GRASSCRETE *(left) is good for areas that have to take vehicles occasionally. The grass grows through the gaps in the concrete so that only a faint impression of the concrete is visible.*

PEBBLES *(right) look good with water features and combine well with gravel, driftwood and one or two sculptural plants. Choose those sold as 'river washed' for the smoothest surface texture.*

WOODEN LOGS, *stripped and stained, are less formal than decking, but not as rustic as untreated logs. There are many different coloured stains available.*

A TEMPERATE MEADOW *is easy to establish. Plant small plants (these are simpler* *than seeds) in bare soil or in a cleared patch of lawn. Fill in gaps later with suitable grass seed.*

UNTREATED WOODEN LOGS *(left) make a rough surface, ideal for wild gardens; they also work well with gravel.*

DAISIES *may grow in your grass (right) if you mow it monthly instead of weekly. If you find the look too informal, mow a strip around the edge each week.*

COARSE BARK *makes a good surface for woodland-garden paths and mulches shrubs and sculptural plants. Take care if using it with low-growing ground cover as it can smother small plants.*

BARK MULCH *is available in several different textures, all of which are good weed suppressors. A layer some 5cm (2in) thick should be enough to inhibit the growth of most annual weeds.*

CLOVER *(above) gives a green grass-like effect, enriches the soil and can be walked on. Its flowers attract bees so it is not suitable for play areas.*

IVY *is a versatile ground cover for dry or moist shade, where grass may not grow. It cannot be walked on – use a bark mulch path or stepping stones for access.*

THYME *forms an attractive flowering carpet in sandy or gravelly soils, but needs sun to flourish. Bees love its scented flowers and the leaves can be used in cooking. Works well with other rock-garden plants.*

CAMOMILE *(above) has a wonderful scent but does not work in large areas or cold wet sites and cannot take heavy traffic. Requires frequent weeding by hand, but does not need mowing.*

NATURAL SURFACES

A soft surface such as a lawn is ideal for sitting, lying or playing on, and can contribute to the much envied 'English garden' effect – a sweep of cool green lawn set off with perfect shrubs and roses. Lawn grasses are hard-wearing because they grow not from their tips but from their roots, so when you walk on the grass or mow it, you do not damage the plant.

If you look after your lawn by mowing it regularly in the growing season, it will have a sprinkling of weeds, but will not look untidy and will be suitable for the children to play on. But a perfect lawn is hard work to achieve. You need to remove weeds by hand or with chemicals, rake to remove the old grass that has formed a thatch, top dress with fine topsoil and sand to keep it level, and feed and water regularly in the growing season.

If you want to use other natural materials, you may find wood practical – in the form of wooden logs, bark mulch or decking. Bark is good for paths and helps to keep the soil moist under new plantings. Decking is a good, relatively inexpensive way to extend the house into the garden, but it can become slippery when wet.

MEADOWS *of naturalised prairie plants (left) need only one mowing in autumn, once the flowers have died down. Suitable plants include black-eyed susans, ox-eye daisies and purple coneflowers.*

DECKING *(right) is a warm, attractive surface which gives a clean, uncluttered look. Ideal for terraces, bridges, steps and paths, it can be laid in long sweeps or crisscross geometric designs. Works well in water gardens.*

COMBINATIONS *of hard and soft surfaces (below), such as grass with gravel, stone and rocks, are popular in Japanese-style gardens and for many people the most practical solution when choosing surface materials.*

DECKING *(left), particularly when used in large expanses, may need its clean, sharp lines softened with containers filled with cheerful, colourful plants such as begonias. It can be left in its natural state or stained many different colours with wood preservative.*

USING SURFACE MATERIALS

A paved patio – an essential for many gardens – is probably the most expensive single element you will choose. If your budget is tight, remember that even if you intend to eat on the patio, the only place you really need hard paving is under the table and chairs; you can extend this hard surface with gravel, which combines well with paving and can be attractive in its own right.

Paths usually work best if they are constructed from the same material as the patio. They should be wide enough – at least 1m (3ft) – for plants to spill on to without causing an obstruction. This can prove costly – a long path can cover a surprisingly large area. Again, gravel is a cheaper option but it needs a retaining edging strip which should be high enough to prevent gravel spilling on to the lawn.

Stepping stones are another economical alternative, and perfect for little-used paths in particular. They also have a softer effect than the more definite line of a path. Stepping stones can be made from concrete, stone or brick and, ideally, should tone with the existing paving. Take care over how far apart you place them – lay them out and try walking from one to the next before you finalise their position.

Steps can create all manner of effects in your garden – they can be narrow and

**CHANGES IN
LEVEL** *need special
treatment. If you have a
change of three steps or
more, consider building
planting terraces
(similar to raised beds,
but not free standing)
on either side of them.
These make small
attractive beds, easy to
maintain, which can be
used for rockery plants* *or herbs, especially if
sited near the kitchen.
Choose brick walls with
brick or tile steps,
drystone walls with
stone steps, or wooden
walls with wood or
gravel steps. Here bricks
and terracotta tiles in
warm tones have been
used, forming an
inviting view which
leads up into the garden.*

steep, enhancing a mysterious effect
as you wonder what lies at the top, or
wide and generous so that you can sit on
them to chat while the children hop up
and down them. A sweep of stone steps
can lead to a balustraded balcony; a
couple of intricate circular brick steps may
fan out on to a lawn. As with paths, you
should choose materials to complement
your paving. It usually works best to have
fewer materials rather than more, which
can look fussy. Do not worry if it looks a
little harsh initially – once the bushes
start to billow in and the plants creep
across, the effect will soon soften.

If you have water in your garden, you
may want a bridge, which can range in
style from a simple wooden plank to an
elaborate ironwork affair. Bridges do not
actually have to span water – you could
make a viewing deck above your pond or
pool with a wide railing to lean on. Your
choice of material – modern lightweight
metal, heavy stone – depends on the
overall effect you are looking for. The
Japanese simply space flat-topped rocks
across the water; these blend well with
rushes and reeds in wildlife gardens.

A BRICK WALL *does not have to be constructed to follow traditional courses.*

Interesting, modern effects can be achieved by setting alternate rows at right angles.

CONCRETE WALLING *cast in semicircles has an open feel. Terracotta walls in*

this style enhance Californian- and Mediterranean-style plantings.

DRYSTONE WALLS *were once common in areas where stone is plentiful. Although*

expensive to lay, they can last for centuries. Plants grow over them and from their crevices.

CAST CONCRETE BLOCKS *are inexpensive, available in many designs and*

easy to install. For a less open appearance, intersperse with blocks of a more solid design.

BOUNDARIES

Walls, hedges and fences usually define a garden's boundaries, but they can also be included within a garden to mark the outline of an enclosure. A low wall or a picket fence can provide an open, welcoming feel to a front garden, as well as forming a boundary for a vegetable patch. At the back and sides of the house, you may prefer something higher or more solid, especially if privacy is a priority.

The most attractive permanent fences can be expensive. Make sure that fence posts are treated against damp and securely fixed in concrete foundations (75cm/30in deep for a 1.8m/6ft fence). Cheaper, less attractive fences can be enhanced by fixing wires to the uprights and training climbers up them.

Hedges can be formal and clipped or informal, made up of large bushes to form a textured line without hard edges. Dig deep and manure the ground before planting to provide a good base for these long-term elements. Walls are commonly made from brick or stone. Concrete is cheaper and available in precast shapes, which can have strong visual effects. Be cautious if you are at all unsure.

COLUMN AND PLINTH *walls made from brick have an open, but rather formal*

appearance. Such structures need professional laying but are long lasting.

LARCHLAP FENCING *is quick and easy to install and inexpensive, but is not long lasting. It can also*

look harsh in large expanses. Plant climbers to soften the effect, but leave room for them to grow.

PICKET FENCING *is ideal for boundaries in rural areas or to surround a cottage-style garden, but less successful in urban gardens. It can be painted or stained a variety of colours.*

INTERWOVEN WATTLE *fencing is short-lived but can look attractive even as it*

decays. Good for cottage and wildlife gardens, it is too irregular for more formal styles.

IRON RAILINGS *are perfect for a smart town house and when properly fixed are long*

lasting, but they need frequent repainting to retain their smart appearance.

TOPIARY *(right) always provides a talking point, adds a touch of humour in the garden and is enjoyable to do if you have the patience – it takes years to train a bird or animal over its wire frame. You can buy topiary shapes ready made at great expense, but all still need frequent trimming.*

KNOT GARDENS *(left) were first popular more than 400 years ago. They were traditionally made from box, as here, or santolina, and filled in with coloured stones. Large public gardens that have such features can be a good source of ideas to try out in your own garden, even if you have to confine your enthusiasms to a more modest scale (inset).*

HEDGES *of holly, yew, laurel or beech work well. Leyland cypresses and lonicera grow quickly.*

IVY *and other trailing plants soften brick walls, but may grow into and weaken old pointing.*

ESPALIER *involves training branches out from a central stem and pinning the tree to a wall.*

SCREENS, GATES AND ARCHES

Trellis or bamboo screens provide lighter, less solid ways to divide the garden than trees or shrubs. Use them to enclose a hidden seat or climbing frame, or to disguise the shed or compost heap. If you want a more substantial division, perhaps between the front and back gardens, or around a tennis court or swimming pool, you can still use trellis, but a high screen must be secured into the ground in the same way as you would stake a fence (see p. 26); it should also be capped with a strong beam along the top.

Pergolas and arches, like steps, can enhance the feel of a garden. Archways tend to be mysterious; they work well with steep narrow steps and high brick walls with locked wooden doors. They can also draw the eye to frame a view. Pergolas originated in Italy and were traditionally covered in grape vines, the perfect setting for long Italian lunches. Such structures are of necessity large. To sit and eat beneath one, if you have a large family, you need a space at least 4 x 4m (13 x 13ft) with an extra 1m (3ft) all around for the pergola itself. Crossbeams above are usually made from wood, but the uprights can be of stone or brick. If you have less space, you could place a smaller pergola over a path, but make it at least 2.3m (7ft 6in) high so that flowers and bunches of grapes can hang inside.

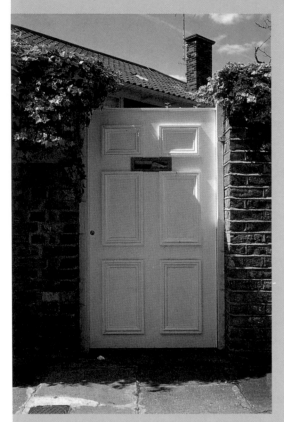

TALL DOORS *in brick walls (above) provide a clue to the style of garden. A mysterious garden would be no surprise behind such an entrance.*

IRON GATES *open on to a path of old red bricks with tile edging, leading to a summerhouse (below). The white paint is echoed in the flowers.*

PERGOLAS *of wood (above and below) look attractive covered in plants, although this takes time to achieve. They must be sturdy enough to support climbers, and can be enhanced if they are painted in a colour to complement the blooms.*

A FINE METAL ARCH *has a minimal effect, ideal for modern gardens. Choose plants to complement the delicate lines.*

PLANT-CLAD ARCHES *of an established pergola provide a shady walk leading to a focal-point statue.*

AN ARCHWAY *in a massive old brick wall shades a fine plain black iron gate, which does not jar with the overall shape.*

STUCCO PIERS, *tall and white, enclose a low dark green gate to create a smart urban entrance.*

CRISSCROSS WOOD *trellis (left) gives an open effect and is suitable for supporting climbers such as roses. It is useful for creating a partial screen, or a light rather than solid enclosure.*

BAMBOO TWIGS *(below), tied at intervals to bamboo horizontals, create an interesting dense screen.*

WATTLE *(right) makes a good rustic-looking screen or fence. It does not stay intact for very long, but is still attractive when old.*

WOODEN TRELLIS *(below) is available in many sizes. Those with small squares have a modern appearance and look good even without plants growing up them.*

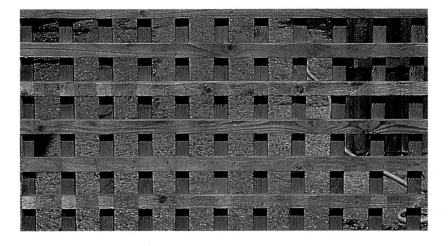

STONE STATUES *often work well in formal gardens and can provide a good focal point. For a more modern garden, you could consider a modern sculpture instead.*

A CLASSICAL FOUNTAIN, *with water cascading down the sides and sparkling in the light, provides a memorable effect, but it needs a garden that is large enough to take it.*

A KIDNEY–SHAPED POOL *(above) set in a stone paved surround lends itself to planting with pink and white water lilies. This is a* relatively new garden, which will be enhanced when the background planting has grown, but even now pool, planting and screens are in harmony.

A RAISED POOL *has an edge that you can sit on. This prefabricated construction has a central fountain and plants in containers in* the water. While the chequered paving and textured wall make the pond the major garden feature, such busyness can detract from the beauty of the water.

PONDS, POOLS AND ORNAMENTS

Water has a powerful effect on a garden, and can add to its interest immeasurably. The style of every water feature should evolve from the design of the garden as a whole. A romantic garden, for example, might have a long stone-edged canal; a cottage garden an old pumphead and stone water trough; in a modern garden you may prefer large rocks and pebbles with water simply running over them. This can be a good choice if you have children, since such features have no standing pool of water into which a child could fall and drown.

In informal gardens, a pond looks more natural if you site it at a low point. If this is impossible, surround it with dense plants to distract the eye from the improbability of its position. And think twice about siting a pond under a tree – you need sun to make the water sparkle, and falling leaves can be a nuisance. Avoid taking the lawn to the pond edge since it will inevitably turn to mud; use gravel, stone or decking, but bear in mind that the last becomes slippery when wet.

To attract wildlife, a pond needs a long curving edge, since the richest life is where water meets land. One edge at least should have a shallow slope so that creatures can wander in and out. Line the bottom with sand, old wool carpet to make a rough surface, and subsoil from your garden – topsoil encourages weeds.

A WILDLIFE POND *supports an incredible variety of life, from the tiniest water-dwelling creatures to birds and bees and other insects* *that are attracted by the flowers. Water lilies offer shade and protection to fish and frogs; marginal plants grow around the edges.*

CONCRETE STEPPING STONES *cleverly continue the path across a stream. Cobbles cover the bottom, reflecting the sun in the water rippling above. At the edges larger cobbles make a link with the concrete surround.*

A PAVILION, *painted white in the colonial style, makes an attractive changing room by the pool. It looks fresh and cool against the blue water and the dark green trees in the background, adding a touch of class to what is otherwise a rather ordinary-looking swimming pool.*

CHECKLIST

FOOD FROM YOUR GARDEN
Growing vegetables and fruit can be hard work, but there is immense satisfaction in eating food from your own garden. A vegetable plot is worth considering if you have the time and will not be on holiday when the crops ripen. Choose your site carefully. Vegetables need not be consigned to the back of the garden, out of sight – many are decorative and attractive, although a plot can look somewhat bare after the harvest.

Tomatoes

Hot tub

If your space is small, use vegetables as you would instant-effect plants – try scarlet runner beans up a trellis, and perhaps red-leafed lettuce as a foliage plant.

Fruit trees can be trained as espaliers (see p. 27) if space is limited; most berrying plants need sun and many require a sheltered spot. Herbs are easy to fit in, either in a self-contained patch or mingled in among the flowers, but they do need a sunny spot, ideally near the kitchen.

LEISURE AND PLAY
With the exception of a hot tub, which can fit into quite a small area, you need space to accommodate leisure equipment for adults. Think about how much – realistically – you might use a swimming pool or tennis court, which may well dominate the garden. Swimming pools, tennis courts, jacuzzis and hot tubs need careful siting and professional installation.

Garden table and chairs

SEATING
For most people, somewhere to sit is a must in the garden and fixed seating can be invaluable. Wood is warmer than metal or stone, although your style may dictate the materials: metal may suit a modern garden; stone is good in mysterious gardens; and cast iron works well in romantic ones.

Cast iron garden chair

The obvious place for tables and chairs is on the patio or terrace, but this is not the only site. Try putting a seat or bench in a corner that gets the winter sun; not only will this provide a good focal point – you will be surprised at how often you use it.

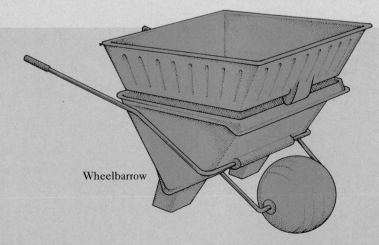

Wheelbarrow

UTILITY ITEMS
Do you also need a toolshed (a lawn mower may fit into a cupboard); compost bin; clothes line; rubbish bins; fixed barbecue? A clothes line must be in the sun, but ideally out of sight too. The barbecue needs to be close to kitchen and patio if possible.

Beans

Strawberries

Sandpit

LIGHTING

An underused magic, lighting can transform a garden, not only when the weather is warm and you sit out at night, but also when you look out of the window on a dull day.

Spotlights are useful for security and practical in utility areas but otherwise can be too glaring and may annoy your neighbours. Consider instead some of the softer light fittings available (manufacturers' catalogues can be invaluable when you are trying to decide what you would like). Generally, low lights are good for lighting paths, uplighters better for silhouetting trees and glow lights perfect behind such plants as ferns.

It is a good idea to have your garden wired with several plug-in sockets so that you can try out lights in various positions to determine where they will give you the effect you want. Many such sockets are fixed to stakes which can simply be pushed into the ground. In this way, you can highlight different areas of the garden at different times of the evening, or use light to draw your visitors from one area to the next.

Exciting lighting effects heighten the impact of the plants on a modern urban patio and add to the illusion of space.

🪜 Large items of play equipment for children are not always necessary. Look at how they like to play: if you can make something exciting out of, say, stepping stones leading to a den, your children will enjoy this at home and find the swings and slides at the park a treat.

🪜 A sandpit can be an attractive feature, but a removable plastic container may be more suitable if space is limited. Consult your children when choosing large items of equipment – many think bright colours babyish.

🪑 If you cannot fit in any permanent seating, choose folding chairs that can be packed away at the end of summer. (A couple of folding chairs are useful for extra guests.) If you have trees, consider a hammock in which to while away long sunny afternoons, or fix a bench beneath.

Tree swing and bench seat

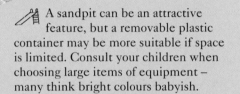

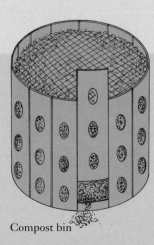

Compost bin

Gardening tools

DEVISING THE PLANTING PLAN

CREATING A PANORAMA

A photograph from an upstairs window may give you too much of an aerial perspective, so stand in the garden near one end of the boundary fence or wall. Stand far enough back to be able to see a reasonable sweep of the boundary and plants in front of it through the lens, but not so far that you lose all detail.

Take a photograph, making sure that you have a recognisable 'landmark' – fence post, red flower, shed door – in the extreme right of the viewfinder. Keeping the camera level, move horizontally down one side of the garden until your landmark is in the extreme left of the viewfinder. Make sure that there is another landmark in the right of the viewfinder, and take this shot. Repeat right around the garden. When you lay your prints out, you will have a broad sweep of garden.

Depending on your garden's size, you may get good results with a panoramic camera that shoots wide narrow images.

With the large hard and soft elements in place, you can start to consider the planting plan more closely. This is also the time to look at height, the third dimension in your plan – what you have worked out with the grid and stickers must work when you use the garden.

The easiest way to visualise exactly how your new garden will look is to take photographs of the areas you are going to plant afresh. Try to overlap them so that you get a panorama and can be sure that all the important elements, such as a shed or large tree, are there.

The problems that exist in the garden below may be reflected to a greater or lesser extent in your own garden. Some have easy solutions; others are more

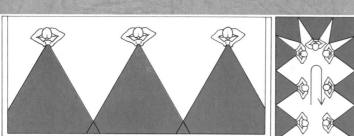

A CONCRETE GARAGE in your own or a neighbour's garden is dull and unsightly.
Solutions: Mask its stark texture with plants and/or screen with a trellis.

A TREE YOU CANNOT MOVE casts shade into your garden, and/or is not to your taste.

difficult to tackle, but bear in mind that the more interesting your garden becomes overall, the less obvious some of these problems will appear.

Read through the rest of this chapter for suggestions on how to treat specific areas: how to use colour; the importance of texture and shape; and tips on choosing plants for particular circumstances or looks. Cut pictures from seed catalogues, magazines and garden centre catalogues and position them over the elements that you want to change in your garden. If you cannot find what you want elsewhere, cut out pieces of coloured paper. When you have a broad notion of what you want in terms of colour and general attributes, use the *Plant Directory* on pp. 48–65 to narrow down your options.

You may not get the look you want first time, but keep trying. Keep thinking about the style you wanted, and relate that to the grid and stickers plan you devised and the panorama in front of you. Is it all fitting together? If this third dimension is making your plan impractical – if you realise, for example, that a screen is not going to block out the children's swing or that you cannot counterbalance a tall tree with the small shrub you had in mind – go back and alter the arrangement of stickers.

A LOW FENCE may mean that the whole garden is overlooked. *Solution: If this is near the house or seating area, fix trellis to the top and grow climbers over it.*

PLAY EQUIPMENT is not always a must (see pp. 32–33), but if your children do like it, you may want to have a swing or slide. *Solutions: Make the garden more interesting to draw the eye away from the equipment; screen it with trellis; if you are installing play equipment, choose sympathetic materials.*

A WINDOW IN A NEIGHBOUR'S HOME gives a clear view of your garden. *Solution: Screen your seating area so that it, at least, remains private.*

Solutions: Prune overhanging branches to reduce shade; build a shade garden beneath; plant something to lessen the tree's impact.

A GENERALLY BORING SHAPE gives you scope for change. Your garden has 60cm (2ft) beds all around with an untidy round central rosebed – it is difficult to keep round edges neat.

Solution: Complete re-design; perhaps surprisingly, this is one of the easiest problems to deal with since everything is within your control. Start by masking out the rosebed: you will notice an instant improvement.

HOW TO CHOOSE PLANTS

Follow the stages given here in relation to your own garden. Perhaps you have a large bed at the back of the lawn. On one side is the path to the garage. You would like a large shrub to stand in the corner of that bed. List what you need, perhaps *5m (16ft) high/ evergreen/solid/ handsome in winter*. Such a plant does not have to be spectacular in itself, since you can always put a smaller or brighter shrub in front of it, but to look solid in winter, it will almost certainly need to be an evergreen.

Now, you might want a plant to flank that evergreen; perhaps an arching shape would work well, and you would like light-coloured leaves to stand out against the large shrub. This list might say: *deciduous / arching / light foliage – white or yellow variegated / 1.8–2.5m (6–8ft)*. The third major plant in this bed marks the entrance to the path, for which you might consider something low and rounded. With the major elements of the bed planted, you can then add the smaller plants. And, for symmetry, you might decide to repeat your small round shrub on the other side of the path, giving you your first plant for the bed there, and so on.

As you continue to add shrubs, think about the shapes of what is there already. Many large arching shrubs, for example, have a relatively thin base, so there is a lot of space underneath. You could balance this with some lower shrubs, or leave the space open and cover the ground with a carpet of low-growing perennials.

BUILDING UP THE PLANTING

Larger plants, such as trees and shrubs, that form the basic structure of your planting scheme are your first priority after any building work. As many as one-third to half of the structural plants that, together with the hard elements, form the bones of the garden will probably be evergreen. For each plant that you want to put into your garden, draw up a list of desired attributes (see box left), including its main purpose – screening plant, focal point and so on. Then, using the advice given and the *Plant Directory*, you should be able to find the plants to meet your needs.

SCREENING PLANTS

Do you need a screen to hide something or to form an enclosure? If you are trying to block out a distant view, whatever you use will have to be large, so you might need a tree. An upright tree, perhaps one of the conifers, may not be broad enough, so you will need something with a rounded or spreading canopy. Look outside before you decide on a tree: if there are laburnums or rowans in your street, a large purple-leaved plum may be intrusive. Likewise, if there are nothing but palm trees, your glade of silver birches – always supposing you could keep them alive in the heat – may look odd.

Deciduous or evergreen? A deciduous tree will build up a fine network of branches and screen to some extent in winter, too, but will not provide as dense a screen as an evergreen. If you choose a fast-growing species for a screening plant, be sure to check on its final size.

A group of shrubs may work better than a single tree or shrub if your purpose is to enclose a seating area or pool. But if you use a group of large shrubs, you are in effect creating a flowerbed which will need more plants to fill it out.

SCREENS can be formed from plants as well as trellis. Here, a variety of shrubs, clearly defined lawn edge and carefully placed seat instantly draw the eye; the children's swing recedes into the background. A tree of medium height screens the seat from the neighbour's window.

TRELLIS SCREENS *can be used to soften the effect of unsightly walls. Such screens are ideal when you want height without spread, but take care with plant choice against concrete, which reflects hot sun.*

A GROUP OF PLANTS *may need a focus. Cutting back and removing overgrown shrubs has revealed a wine-red specimen, complemented in spring by colourful tulips.*

PLANTS FOR WALLS AND TRELLIS SCREENS

A trellis makes an immediate difference, and if you choose a vigorous climber, you can have a screen of sorts fairly quickly. But trellis screens are open, and do not completely mask the structure behind. They are suitable for such climbers as clematis and honeysuckle which can twine through the structure, but make sure the trellis is strong enough to take the weight. Walls can take more substantial plants such as shrubs, trained flat along wires nailed into a framework. If you train plants up a wall, consider whether it is sunny or shady. Some shrubs that are on the borders of hardiness in temperate zones, such as ceanothus and escallonia, will flourish against a wall that is in the sun for much of the day. But take care with early-morning sun on frosty days: it can scorch the leaves of tender plants. The soil at the base of walls is usually dry, so plant at least 30cm (12in) out from there. Shrubs such as pyracantha and *Garrya elliptica* can be trained on to a shady wall, while a climber like parthenocissus will grow fairly high up a wall by itself. But all may need care at some point, so it is wise to keep whatever you choose trimmed to a height you can reach with a step ladder.

FOCUS PLANTS

Do you want something to view from your window? Or to catch sight of across the lawn? A single beautiful tree such as a delicate Japanese maple with spectacular autumn leaves, or a purple cotinus to glow in the morning sun may be your choice. Do not rule out herbaceous plants – a tall striking flower like crambe can be most effective, as can a grass like *Arundo donax*. You may also want to provide a focal point within a group of plants; this may change, from a brilliant clump of red tulips in spring to the creamy spires of yucca in summer. Try out different plants in the position you want (pots of instants are good for experimentation). Consider both colour and overall shape against the background.

PLANT TERMINOLOGY

These are the categories of plant that will be discussed further in this kit, with notes on what you should consider before you buy.

● *Trees*

These are woody plants with a clearly defined trunk, from which branches spread. They take years to mature and live for a long time, so should not be impulse buys. Think about foliage colour, when it flowers and/or fruits and for how long, and how much shade you want from a tree. Try to look at mature specimens in your area to see how tall they grow and how much they spread.

● *Shrubs*

Woody stems and branches that grow from ground level characterise a shrub. As with trees, consider mature height and spread. Shrubs also have flowers, which on a tall shrub may draw the eye upward.

● *Climbers*

There are several categories of climber, including self clinging, such as ivy, and twining, like honeysuckle. Twining climbers need a trellis or screen to cling to.

● *Ground cover*

The layer of planting below shrubs is referred to as ground cover. These plants often work best if they are used with some idea of their natural habitat. Four basic ecological categories have been used.

Woodland plants generally grow best in shade in moist or cool conditions. *Woodland-edge plants* grow under the overhang of trees or shrubs, or in bright sunny clearings in woodland. *Open-ground plants* originate in damp meadows, dry grassland or on sandy heaths. They grow best with similar species. *Rock plants* are ideal for stony situations, such as formal rock gardens, and in paving and gravel.

● *Annuals*

These are planted, flower, set seed and die in one season. Some plants used as annuals are in fact perennial (living for a few years) in some areas and can be used as ground cover.

STYLES OF PLANTS

When you are choosing plants to add to your basic structure, keep in mind the attributes and shapes of what is there already – evergreen or deciduous; rounded, spreading or upright. Work systematically – plant more shrubs first, then the ground cover, providing depth to the effect you are looking for.

If you are not sure what you are trying to say with your plants, think about those garden styles in chapter one that you did not like. Was the wildlife garden too untidy and messy for you? You probably like a more formal look – compact, low-growing hedges and easily managed ground cover. Was the instant one too bright and garish? If you prefer more muted shades, you may have found the romantic garden more appealing. You will find that you already have some idea of what you do like, if only by reference to what you do not.

Reactions to plants are highly subjective, so be prepared for strong

SINISTER PLANTS are faintly threatening even if, like Garrya elliptica, they are tall, dark and distinguished. This handsome shrub has slightly metallic evergreen leaves and elegant cream tassels in winter and early spring (in high winds these may get tangled, which tends to spoil the effect).

responses to your garden – both positive and negative. To some, Shasta daisies are the perfect cottage-garden plant; whereas others only note their funereal whiteness. And while some people are drawn to the fragrance of *Choisya ternata*, others find its aroma too pungent and overpowering.

Typically, romantic plants are powerfully scented, like roses or regal lilies (though lilies can also have funereal connotations), or double and frothy, like paeonies. If you want a sinister feeling in a dark corner, try a poisonous aconitum, or a hellebore with its dramatic pointy leaves, or the threatening prickles of a gaunt *Mahonia lomarifolia*.

For a mysterious garden, look for a delicate pendent flower, like dicentra, or choose the feathery blooms of cimicifuga.

ROMANTIC for both its lovely hanging flowers and its foliage, wisteria (left) is at its best twining around a Gothic window.

MYSTERIOUS and shadowy, Hydrangea sargentiana (right) grows prolifically. Its large lacecap flowers edged in white have a ghostly appearance in the shade.

You could also consider something white, perhaps a lacecap hydrangea.

Bright friendly plants in primary colours, such as daisies, marigolds and sunflowers, are jolly. You could also choose anything with bright autumn berries, such as *Skimmia japonica* or *Sorbus* 'Joseph Rock', or a plant that produces attractive flowers and fruit like *Chaenomeles*, the Japanese quince. Many annuals fall into this category and a garden filled with them is welcoming and cheerful.

Sculptural plants fit particularly well into modern or minimalist gardens,

although they can enhance many plantings. Such a plant may well be your first choice to create a focus, something that immediately draws the eye.

'Over-grand' is perhaps the most subjective attribute of all. Some people could not imagine a garden without rhododendrons for their massive flower effect; others think that they really belong in large plantings. And there is something of a herd instinct among gardeners at times, with certain plants becoming over-used and over-popular, which may go against your natural taste. Remember, however, that many of these plants have become popular simply because they are reliable and fit many different styles of garden. In addition, it is not the plant itself but rather the way it is used that creates originality. Follow your instincts about what you put into your garden – the chances are you will be right.

SCULPTURAL *plants make an impact. With huge oval silver-haired leaves held upright by a basal rosette,* Verbascum bombyciferum *(left) is striking and dramatic. It works best sparsely planted in dry rocky areas, perhaps surrounded by gravel.*

JOLLY PLANTS *enliven any garden.* Gaillardia *'Goblin' (right) only grows to some 35cm (14in) high, but there are many other varieties, in sunny reds and golds, all flowering all summer long. These plants originally came from the prairies of North America, and like long dry summers. They do best in sandy soil in open situations.*

FLOWER AND FOLIAGE COLOUR

AGAINST A DARK BACKGROUND
Cotinus coggygria 'Royal Purple' glows. This can be a dazzling shrub, but it must be placed well – either as here with starlike white flowers to enhance its colour and the light catching its leaves, or silhouetted so that the translucence of the foliage can be seen.

Most gardens can take only one dark red shrub; too many make the effect dismal and dark. Bright colours or white bring out the drama of cotinus best.

Before you start to build up your planting plan, consider the colours of other elements in the garden – the grey of stones, the cream of concrete, the sandy yellow or red of bricks. You may wish to complement them with harmonious tones, adding warm golds and oranges to your yellow brick wall, or to make a contrast, with bright pink helianthemums sprawling over your grey stone paving. Remember, too, that green is a colour, so a green lawn makes a strong accent that needs taking into account.

Strong colours like red and orange draw the eye; pale colours such as pale yellow, blue and white recede and are useful for making the garden look longer than it is, so plant bright colours close to the house and lighter shades toward the

✳ PERFUME

Any spot that holds the heat will bring out the fragrance of perfumed plants, and perfume enhances any garden.
Roses come first for flower scent, especially the rugosa and musk varieties; several of the climbers are also fragrant, including the honeysuckle *Lonicera japonica* 'Halliana' and summer jasmine. You could also try plants such as sweet alyssum (honey), *Cytisus battandieri* (pineapple), lilac, philadelphus (orange blossom), viburnum and daphne. For scented foliage consider *Cistus x purpureus, Choisya ternata* and box.

***Lavender's** fragrance is unmistakable.*

back. Pale colours look ghostly and ethereal against dark shady backgrounds, while brilliant reds and oranges glow like jewels. Areas of similar colours – strong or pale – tend to work best together, but you can break this rule if you wish: in a pink and white planting some self-seeded orange poppies might look irresistible.

Colour does not simply mean flower colour. Leaves may be on the plant all year, flowers for a few weeks at most. Start by thinking about foliage colour. Bright green is most common in temperate climates, but can look out of place under a hot dry sun, where grey or perhaps dark green may be more at home. Start from these basics and move outward.

Against a green background you could add yellow variegation for a warm sunny effect, especially in shady borders, or white for a quieter look. Yellow variegated plants can take the sun, but all-yellow or white variegated leaves scorch and prefer shade.

Rich reds and purples can be exciting foliage colours, but need sun to shimmer; they look good with grey or blue-grey, or with the reddish green of *Euphorbia griffithii* 'Great Dixter'. Most grey-leaved plants like sun and look wonderful in the evening light and in autumn, especially mixed with white, pale blues and yellows. Those that prefer shade, such as *Hosta sieboldiana* and *Dicentra* 'Pearl Drops', can be mysterious and enhance a place to sit alone and listen to the sounds of evening.

Dark greens on their own can be sombre, perhaps demanding a blast of red.

When you come to add the flowers, similar colours deepen an effect, so hot reds and oranges will reinforce the warmth of yellow foliage. Add misty blue or white if you wish to tone it down. Think of the overall mood you want – if elegant,

TECHNICOLOUR BRILLIANCE *is achieved by combining acid yellows and warm and burnt oranges against grey-white tanacetum. Use such mixes for containers and sunny window boxes. Or create a bright display in the garden, perhaps harmonised with more reds and tawny tones, or cooled down with blue flowers and more grey foliage.*

you could try silver-blue *Helictotrichon sempervirens* with purple allium and deep red roses; black ophiopogon behind a luscious green fern with sprays of pink astilbe may give a sinister effect.

In general, if you use flowers and foliage of the same tone, with one or two contrasts, it works better than a colourful mix, which can look garish and muddled. When you bring home impulse buys that do not really suit your scheme, try the pots out in different places to see where they fit best. Do not dot 'colour interest' all over the garden and beware of too much variegation – bright colours can look busy and restless, pale shades anaemic.

SHAPE AND TEXTURE

GLOSSY AND SHINY, *the leaves of* Camellia japonica *'Kimberley' are complemented by pillar-box red flowers in spring. Because of their attractive leaves, camellias look good on their own in containers, with nothing to detract from their stature. Most varieties are solid and rounded in shape.*

Colour should not be considered in isolation from leaf shape and texture, since leaves contribute a great deal to the character of a plant and the impact it will have on your garden.

Texture alters the effect of leaf colour. Shiny laurel or gardenia leaves catch the light, producing a lustrous shine; narrow dark green leaves, like those of rosemary, trap light and are matt. Some leaves (such as hosta) have a ridged texture; others are furry (*Ballota pseudodictamnus*, for example, is good in gardens for the blind or partially sighted as its leaves are lovely to stroke). In shape, plants can be soft and rounded like potentilla, spiky like yucca, or grass-like such as hemerocallis.

Draw up your desired plant attributes (see p. 36). If your list says rounded, do you want something soft like a *Viburnum tinus* or spiny like an osmanthus? If you are aiming for solidity, holly may be better than a hydrangea. Lower-growing rounded plants such as *Hebe rakaiensis* can provide rhythm and emphasis in a bed.

FINE SILKY HAIRS *clothe the oval leaves of* Stachys byzantina *'Silver Carpet' (above left), which does not flower. The more sun it has, the more silvery the plant becomes. A marvellous fast-growing ground cover, this species does not like damp in winter, since wet rots the leaves.*

THE FEATHERY SPIKES *of* Astilbe chinensis *'Pumila' rise above its ferny green foliage (above), which makes good dense ground cover for deep shade. Plant it in moist soil with other woodland plants, such as hosta, aconitum and the grass Deschampsia caespitosa.*

SLENDER GRASSY *foliage and dainty inky-purple flowers are the striking features of* Iris sibirica *which, despite its graceful look, is very tough. It originates in damp meadows and swamps but is equally at home in drier soil.*

WITH ITS SOFT AND ROUNDED *clumps of the deepest blue, this mophead hydrangea grows best in damp, partly shaded conditions and cannot take dryness. Such depth of colour is most often seen in sunny climes.*

Tall billowing plants can be grand and stately like *Magnolia grandiflora*. Similar in effect are rhododendrons, but here the texture of the leaves is much duller. This is why clumps of rhododendrons can be heavy and depressing when they are not in flower. You can lighten them with the bright green lushness of ferns or the fine flowers of lacecap hydrangeas. Arching plants are soft and delicate, often – as in *Buddleia alternifolia* – with fine willow-like leaves which sway in the breeze.

Spiky species that stab the sky with pointed leaves can either stand out in a sea of grasses or be grouped together with similar rigid plant forms, which can give the whole garden a wild, almost desert-like appearance. Grasses en masse have something of the same wild look. The smaller grasses (and grass-like herbaceous plants) usually need to be repeated several times throughout a planting, but the larger ones make enough of an impact to stand on their own.

SPIKY MOUNDS *of* Yucca gloriosa *'Bright Edge' boldly mark a curve in the path. Yuccas are sculptural plants, often used in powerful contrast to spreading or creeping ground cover. Flower spikes of whitish bell-shaped flowers towering above the sword-shaped leaves add to the drama. The plants like hot dry climates similar to those of their native dunes and rocky hillsides.*

ARCHING AND GRACEFUL Deutzsia magnifica *'Rochester' is an obliging plant, easy to care for and good-looking even when it is not in flower. It has the advantage of being covered in double white flowers at the height of summer when many other shrubs have finished flowering.*

For best effect, plant spreading woodland-edge species beneath it, such as the white foamflower Tiarella cordifolia *or the beautiful blue forget-me-not* Brunnera macrophylla.

SEASONAL INTEREST

In a well-designed garden, the structure of the planting is attractive even when it is not in flower, but if you do want flowers all year, it is sensible to consider autumn and winter first. Plants that flower in winter – heathers, viburnums, hellebores, *Prunus autumnalis* and the lime-green *Euphorbia characias* – often have long-lasting flowers.

For autumn flowers, consider asters, chrysanthemums, achillea (which starts flowering in high summer) and the long-flowering hydrangeas and fuchsias. Try plants that change colour spectacularly, such as parthenocissus, and some berrying and fruiting species. With an almost infinite choice of summer flowers, and bulbs for spring, a flower garden packed with year-round interest is easier to create than you might have imagined.

Pyracantha *grows in sun or shade and has creamy spring flowers (right), orange or scarlet autumn berries (left) and glossy evergreen leaves.*

FILLING IN THE SPACES

plants fall into this category and, grouped together, can form an attractive display in one season. The advantage of annuals is that you can change them from year to year, both the colours you choose and the bed in which you plant them. If you like an effect, you can repeat it next year.

Your local garden centre will have a vast selection of these plants. Since these grow so quickly, it is more economical to

A HEAVENLY MIX *of annuals – larkspur, coreopsis, gaillardia, pansies and pinks – forms an idyllic cloud of colour. This effect is probably achieved only* *by sowing seeds directly on to the soil, which means that for a couple of months the area may have looked bare. The combination works well in cottage gardens.*

Regardless of style, you may find that you have sparse areas in your beds once the main plants are in place. Newly planted shrubs and trees can look stark, and ground cover may need filling out until it becomes established. You may also find that some of your hard or soft areas look rather large and bare. In these situations, you need fillers – and the most popular choices are usually annuals, containers, areas of gravel or stone enhanced with plants, or a combination.

INSTANT PLANTS

Many plants can be used for a quick but relatively short-lived display. The common perception of annuals is that they are brightly coloured, and indeed many are, but plenty of grey-leaved

BRIGHT BEDDING PLANTS *grouped in pots around a beautiful old stone bird bath make an intriguing corner. Interestingly, this container garden, although vibrant and cheerful with the colours of the flowers standing out like jewels against the deep leafy background, contains elements of the mysterious. Where does the path beyond the turquoise gate lead? What surprises are around the bushes?*

buy them as tiny plant strips or to seed your own, either where you want them to bloom or in a greenhouse first. Many of these species seed themselves, in beautiful and unexpected – and sometimes unwanted – places. Keep them well watered and clip them back if they get straggly. That apart, these are easy-care plants.

CONTAINER PLANTS

Annuals can be used to fill up your containers quickly and easily, but you can use more permanent plants such as dwarf trees and shrubs if you wish. (A traditional container plant in cottage gardens was the houseleek – *Sempervivum* – which can last for years.) ' For permanent container plantings, be realistic about how often you are going to be able to water your plants. In summer you may need to do so twice a day.

If watering is going to be difficult, use as large a container as possible and choose drought-resistant species such as lavender and *Phlomis fruticosa*. Box, bay and hydrangeas (the last need plenty of water) are traditional container plants and do well in shade, as do *Fatsia japonica* and bamboo. You can also plant vegetables, herbs and fruit in containers, although you will usually get a smaller yield than if you grow them in the ground.

Lime-haters such as rhododendrons and camellias will not tolerate alkaline soil; if you want them in your garden, you can grow them in acid soil in containers. Water them with rainwater, rather than hard tap water.

IN THE GRAVEL SPACES between the paving in this courtyard garden, sculptural plants thrive. All have been chosen for their architectural forms and habits of growth. Fennel and verbascum love the heat reflected from the stones, and the leaves of Alchemilla mollis form a soft mound. Statuesque miscanthus grass and ligularia complete the effect.

GRAVEL AND STONE GARDENS

This is an ideal way to grow those plants that like their roots cool and shaded, but their heads in the sun. Artemisia, yucca, opuntia (if you have the space), perovskia, allium and eremurus; alpines such as rock pinks and veronicas; and herbs such as rosemary, chives, oregano, mint, thyme and sage, all make ideal stone or gravel plants. A major advantage of gravel is that it drains well, so it suits all those plants that rot if they get too damp.

Prepare a base for the plants, using a mixture of fine gravel (for drainage), sand and loam to a depth of at least 15cm (6in) and then lay your gravel or stones. Root plants in the spaces between the stones or clear a space in the gravel for planting and then take the gravel right up to the plant stems.

Gravel and stone, both of which are available in many shades of brown and grey, can be used as gardens in their own right and are particularly suited to small plots, or front gardens where access may be your first priority. But they are also an attractive and inexpensive way to extend a brick or stone patio. This can be useful if you need somewhere to walk across more or less constantly, and can make a good transition between a paved area and a planted space. If you use only gravel, use a retaining strip to prevent chips spilling on to the lawn, add some stepping stones to walk across, and let the plants crowd in.

PLANTS FOR WILDLIFE GARDENS

DRAGONFLIES *in the Pacific Northwest feed on yarrow. Yarrow is often included in wildflower seed mixes for meadows, but you may find that it is too invasive.*

TORTOISESHELL BUTTERFLIES *sip nectar from* Sedum spectabile *flowers. This species lays its eggs on nettles; later it is attracted to lavender and buddleias.*

Attracting wildlife to your garden depends on two factors – the food you provide by way of plants, and the shelter you can offer from the weather and predators. To attract small insects – which may seem insignificant, but which are vital in the food chain – you usually need native plants. Fruit- and berry-eating birds and small mammals are less fussy.

The richest wildlife occurs where two habitats meet – so the woodland edge and pond edge will be attractive to many species. For a woodland edge in temperate areas, consider hawthorn, holly, rowan, dogrose and honeysuckle, underpinned with bluebells, wood anemones and foxgloves. In an acid area, try native species which might include phlox, wild bleeding heart, merrybells, bloodroot, trout lilies and ferns. Consider dogwoods and mountain laurels in the shrub layer.

A meadow or prairie garden will attract butterflies and bees. Soft blues and pinks are typical of northern meadows, in contrast to the bright, vibrant shades of Australia and the Midwestern prairies, for example. Almost regardless of where you live, such habitats are not difficult to maintain, but buy a wildflower gardening book to get you started.

Deserts, mountains, swamps and dry steppes all have their own flora and fauna and your local wildlife association can provide information on what to plant, what you can hope to entice into your garden – and how to maintain it. Once you have done the planting, it is best to leave well alone – a wildlife garden does not need constant tidying.

PLANTS FOR PONDS AND POOLS

You have two basic options if you want water in your garden – a clean-water pool or a balanced-life pond. A clean-water pool such as a swimming pool needs aerating with a fountain or filter, frequent skimming of the leaves and dust that gather on its surface and cleaning with a chemical or saline system. A fountain with a stone basin is a lot less work.

If you want plants to grow in the water, you need to develop a balanced-life pool. A formal lily pond will create its own balance, in time supporting a healthy range of frogs, snails and even newts, but be prepared to wait.

A good mix of the different types of water plants is essential. Start with some submerged oxygenating plants. The most commonly sold of these is Canadian pondweed (*Elodea canadensis*), but it is very invasive and best avoided unless you have a large expanse of water. For a smaller pond, consider *Myriophyllum spicatum*, *Potamogeton crispus* or callitriche. Emergent plants such as arrowhead and lesser reed mace send their erect stems high above the water, while water lilies are free floating. To prevent them from becoming invasive, confine their roots to large submerged pots. They then spread out their leaves and flowers on the surface, offering shade and cover for pond creatures. Marginal plants grow at the edges of the pond. Among such plants, consider yellow iris, which can be invasive, pale blue

THE FLAT PADS *of water lilies float to the surface of a pond, providing cool shade for the water organisms below and platforms on which many species of insects can court and mate. Do not make a pond too small if you want to include a good range of water plants, and remember that marshy plants such as grasses and reeds around the pond will help to blend it into the surrounding garden.*

water forget-me-not (*Myosotis scorpioides*) and water mint, which butterflies love.

If space permits, create a damp area around your pond, planting marshy species such as meadowsweet with its scented fluffy white flowers, hemp agrimony (*Eupatorium cannabinum*) and yellow loosestrife. Plants that do well in wetlands include swamp milkweed, blue water hyssop (*Bacopia caroliniana*), bog rosemary (*Andromeda glaucophylla*) and the American swamp lily (*Crinum americanum*).

A swimming pool should be enclosed for safety – use a gate that can be locked if you have children – and you may want to screen it from the house with a trellis or hedge. (The same considerations as for other screens apply, see pp. 36–37.) If your pool area is big enough, you can plant a whole swimming pool garden around the pool itself, softening the glaring brightness of the pool with lush green tropical-looking bushes such as *Fatsia japonica*, some bamboos and a gigantic *Gunnera manicata*. Create a separate shady area in which to sit, surrounded by ferns and cool greenery, under a pergola overhung with trailing wisteria or trumpet vine. Alternatively, try pampas grass or *Arundo donax*. If you have sandy soil, consider a running grass such as *Leymus arenarius*, which will form a shimmering blue river, but contain it in one large planting so that it cannot take over completely.

Campanula carpatica, p. 50

SYMBOLS

Light

☼ full sun

☀ partial shade

✹ complete shade

Minimum winter temperature tolerated

◈ 0°C (32°F)

◈ -5°C (23°F)

◈ -15°C (5°F)

◈ frost tender, see temperature given

Soil

◖ well drained

◗ moist

◗ wet

pH prefers acid soil

Other features

✳ fragrant or aromatic

❀ attracts bees, butterflies or other insects

Ceanothus 'Blue Mound'

Throughout the plant directory species are grouped according to colour – blue and purple, red and pink, yellow and orange, white and cream, and green and grey. Within those broad groups, plants are divided into trees, shrubs and climbers – the basic bone-structure plants (see pp. 36–37); plants and bulbs for ground cover and display, with an indication of the ecological subgroup to which they belong, if appropriate (see box, p. 37); and annuals, which are planted afresh each summer. Some of these technically may be perennials and will last for three or four years where the climate allows, but all are sold as annuals. Species have been included for both flowers and foliage and are listed under the colour of the feature that is of most interest.

The cultivation preferences of a species are shown by symbols (left). Heights and spreads are maximums. If other colours are available, this is listed at the end of an entry.

BLUE AND PURPLE

TREES, SHRUBS AND CLIMBERS

Abutilon x suntense 'Violetta'

☼ ◈ ◖

A fast-growing arching deciduous shrub that can be trained against a wall. It has green foliage, and purple flowers in early summer.

Ht. 5m (16ft); spr. 3m (10ft)

Alygogyne huegelii

Blue hibiscus

☼ ◈ ◖

This shrub bears blue or lilac satin-like hibiscus-shaped flowers and deeply indented leaves. It blooms intermittently year round.

Ht. 2.5m (8ft); spr. 1.2m (4ft)

Bougainvillea glabra

☼ ◈ ◖

Grown on every Mediterranean villa, this vigorous twining climber has round to oval leaves and deep purple flowers in summer.

Min. winter temp. 7–10°C (45–50°F)
Ht. 1.5m (5ft)
Also red/pink, white

Buddleia 'Lochinch'

☼ ◈ ◖ ◗ ❀

A fast-growing arching deciduous shrub with attractive grey foliage, and pale purple flower plumes in late summer. Hybrids with deep purple flowers are also available.

Ht. and spr. 3m (10ft)
Also red, white

Caryopteris x clandonensis 'Heavenly Blue'

☼ ◈ ◖

This deciduous shrub is rounded in shape, has green foliage and blue flowers. Prune back hard in spring.

Ht. and spr. 1m (3ft)

Ceanothus

☼ ◈ ◈ ◖

A genus of rounded bushy evergreen and deciduous shrubs, most flowering in early summer. All are ideal for giving the garden shape, and can be trained against walls.

C. 'Blue Mound' is evergreen with glossy leaves and deep blue flowers in late spring.
Ht. 1.5m (5ft); spr. 2m (6½ft)

C. 'Gloire de Versailles' has racemes of pale blue flowers in summer and autumn and mid-green foliage.
Ht. and spr. 1.5m (5ft)

C. thyrsiflorus var. repens is rounded, low-growing and evergreen with pale blue flowers in early summer.
Ht. 1m (3ft); spr. 2.5m (8ft)

Ceratostigma willmottianum

☼ ◈ ◖

A deciduous low-growing shrub with deep blue flowers from late summer to autumn, and good autumn foliage.

Ht. and spr. 1m (3ft)

Chamaecyparis pisifera 'Boulevard'

Sawara cypress

☼ ☀ ✹ ◈ ◖ ◗

This conical conifer with horizontal branches is of most interest for its blue-silver foliage.

Ht. 15m (50ft); spr. 5m (16ft)

Clematis

☼ ☀ ◈ ◖

A genus of mainly deciduous twining climbers which thrive in lime soils. Some like sun on their flowers, but all need their roots in shade – use stones if necessary. Good for trellises and screens, cottage and romantic gardens.

Also pink/red, white

C. alpina has bell-shaped clear blue flowers in spring.
Ht. 3m (10ft); spr. 1.5m (5ft)

C. 'Jackmanii', with large purple flowers in late summer, is fast-growing and easy to cultivate.
Ht. 3m (10ft); spr. 1m (3ft)

C. 'Perle d'Azur' has large pure blue flowers in summer.
Ht. 3m (10ft); spr. 1m (3ft)

C. viticella has late-flowering violet-purple blooms.
Ht. 4m (13ft); spr. 1.5m (5ft)

Cobaea scandens

☼ ◈ ◖

The summer flowers of this twining climber are green, but turn

Eucalyptus niphophila

purple with age and last to the first frosts.

Min. winter temp. 4°C (39°F)
Ht. 5m (16ft)

Convolvulus tricolor 'Heavenly Blue'

☼ ◈ ◖

A fast-growing twining climber with bright blue flowers in summer and autumn.

Ht. 3m (10ft)
Also white

Eucalyptus gunnii

Cider gum

☼ ◈ ◖

This evergreen tree is grown for its foliage – silver-blue in young specimens, blue-green in more mature ones.

Ht. 27m (90ft); spr. 10m (33ft)

E. niphophila

Snow gum

☼ ◈ ◖

This evergreen tree has silver-blue foliage and white flowers.

Ht. 10m (33ft); spr. 6m (15ft)

Felicia amelloides 'Santa Anita'

Blue marguerite

☼ ◈ ◖

An evergreen bushy spreading shrub with

Jacaranda mimosifolia

Salvia officinalis
'Purpurascens'

daisy-like blue flowers with bright yellow centres from late spring to autumn. Does not tolerate wet.

Ht. and spr. 30cm (12in)

Hardenbergia comptoniana

☼ ❖ ♢

The flowers of this spring-blooming evergreen twining climber are like those of a pea plant and deep purple-blue.

Ht. 2.5m (8ft)

Heliotropium arborescens

☼ ❖ ♢

This evergreen shrub bears purple flowers from spring to the end of autumn.

Min. winter temp. 7°C (45°F)
Ht. 70cm (27in); spr. 1m (3ft)

Hibiscus syriacus 'Blue Bird'

☼ ❖ ♢

Ideal for cottage gardens, this deciduous shrub bears large lilac-blue flowers in summer and autumn.

Ht. 3m (10ft); spr. 2.5m (8ft)
Also pink, white

Hydrangea

☼ ✳ ❖ ♢

A genus of shrubs and climbers, all of which have flower heads consisting of many small flowers. In acid soils, flowers are blue; elsewhere they vary.

Also red/pink, white

H. aspera is a deciduous upright shrub bearing flowers from summer to mid-autumn. In acid soils, the flower heads vary in colour from blue or deep purple for the small inner ones to large and white, or pink tinged, for the outer. Good for mysterious gardens.

Ht. 2.5m (8ft); spr. 2m (6½ft)

H. a. sargentiana is similar but has large rounded furry leaves and is gaunt in shape – good for sinister or mysterious gardens.

Ht. 2.5m (8ft); spr. 2m (6½ft)

H. macrophylla is a dense bushy shrub with glossy green leaves. Mophead forms such as 'Blue Bonnet' have large round flowers; lacecaps, including 'Blue Wave', are similar to *H. aspera*. These are good for both romantic and cottage gardens.

Ht. 2m (6½ft); spr. 2.5m (8ft)

Jacaranda mimosifolia

☼ ❖ ♢

This fast-growing deciduous tree bears clusters of bright blue to blue-purple flowers in spring and summer.

Min. winter temp. 7°C (45°F)
Ht. 12m (40ft); spr. 8.5m (28ft)

Juniperus horizontalis 'Blue Chip'

Creeping juniper

☼ ✳ ❖ ♢

A good ground-cover species with feathery blue-grey foliage.

Ht. 30cm (12in); spr. 1.2m (4ft)

Lavandula angustifolia 'Hidcote'

Lavender

☼ ❖ ♢ ✳ ❀

Good in romantic and cottage gardens, this shrub has silver leaves and purple flowers.

Ht. and spr. 70cm (27in)
Also pink, white

Passiflora caerulea

Blue passion flower

☼ ◈ ♢

The flowers of this evergreen twining

Wisteria sinensis

climber have blue- or purple-banded crowns.

Ht. 10m (33ft)

Perovskia atriplicifolia 'Blue Spire'

☼ ❖ ♢ ✳

Spikes of violet-blue flowers adorn the grey-white stems of this deciduous shrub in summer and autumn.

Ht. 1.2m (4ft); spr. 1m (3ft)

Rhododendron 'Blue Peter'

☼ ✳ ❖ ♢ pH

In early summer this bushy evergreen has

funnel-shaped lavender flowers with frilled petal edges.

Ht. and spr. 4m (13ft)

Rosa 'Blue Moon'

☼ ❖ ♢ ✳

Probably the best of the few 'blue' roses, this bush variety has large silvery-lilac to lavender flowers which last all summer and into autumn. Its foliage is also attractive. Can be grown in containers.

Ht. 1m (3ft); spr. 60cm (24in)

Salvia officinalis 'Purpurascens'

Sage

☼ ❖ ♢

This bushy shrub has purple-tinged leaves when young; they turn silver and are edible. Summer flowers are purple or blue-purple.

Ht. 60cm (24in); spr. 30cm (12in)

Sollya heterophylla

Bluebell creeper

☼ ❖ ♢

The bell-shaped sky blue flowers of this

evergreen twining climber are borne in clusters of up to nine and bloom from spring to autumn.

Ht. 3m (10ft)

Syringa 'Katherine Havemeyer'

Lilac

☼ ❖ ♢ ✳

One of the classic cottage-garden shrubs, this has deep purple-lavender flowers which grow in dense cone-shaped clusters.

Ht. and spr. 5m (16ft)
Also pink, white

Tibouchina urvilleana

Glory bush

☼ ❖ ♢ pH

This evergreen shrub has clearly veined leaves and clusters of shiny purple-blue flowers.

Min. winter temp. 7°C (45°F)
Ht. 3m (10ft); spr. 2.5m (8ft)

Vitex agnus–castus

Chaste tree

☼ ❖ ♢ ✳

This deciduous shrub bears upright panicles of violet flowers in autumn; its leaves are dark green.

Ht. and spr. 2.5m (8ft)

Wisteria sinensis

☼ ❖ ♢ ✳

Racemes of pale purple flowers bloom in early summer and sometimes again in autumn on this deciduous twining climber. This is an ideal plant for pergolas, walls and trellises, but if you are growing it over a pergola leave at least 30cm (12in) for the flowers to hang down.

Ht. 9m (33ft)

PLANTS FOR DISPLAY AND GROUND COVER

Aconitum napellus

Monkshood, helmet flower

☼ ✳ ❖ ♢

Although they prefer sun, these woodland perennials tolerate shade, which enhances the strength of colour of their light indigo hooded flowers. Borne on tall spires, these appear in summer. Good for sinister gardens. Poisonous.

Ht. 1.5m (5ft); spr. 30cm (12in)

Agapanthus campanulatus

☼ ❖ ♢ ♢

In summer this clump-forming perennial bears bright blue flowers in rounded umbels on its strong stems. The leaves of this open-ground plant are grey-green.

Ht. 1.2m (4ft); spr. 50cm (20in)

Allium christophii

Onion

☼ ❖ ♢

This open-ground bulb has a single large umbel of some 50 star-shaped violet-purple flowers in summer. Its leaves are grey.

Ht. 40cm (16in); spr. 20cm (8in)

Agapanthus campanulatus

Brunnera macrophylla

A. sphaerocephalon

☼ ❖ ◌

Umbels of up to 40 bell-shaped pinkish-purple flowers appear on the slender stems of this open-ground bulb in summer.

Ht. 60cm (24in); spr. 10cm (4in)

Anemone blanda 'Atrocaerulea'

☼ ❖ ◌

In early spring this woodland tuber produces daisy-like deep blue flowers, which bear up to 14 narrow petals. Its leaves are deep green and resemble those of geraniums.

Ht. 10cm (4in); spr. 15cm (6in)
Also red, white

Aster novi-belgii 'Lady in Blue'

Michaelmas daisy

☼ ☀ ❖ ◌ ✿

A dwarf hybrid with rich blue flowers.

Ht. and spr. 25cm (10in)
Also red/pink, white

A. sedifolius

☼ ☀ ❖ ◌

This autumn-flowering perennial produces domes of

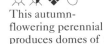

Euphorbia characias subsp.
wulfenii

---

star-shaped lavender-coloured flowers.

Ht. and spr. 50cm (20in)

Aubrieta

☼ ❖ ◌ ✿

There are many varieties of this evergreen trailing rock perennial, in shades of blue, purple, lavender and deep crimson.

Ht. 10cm (4in); spr. 30cm (12in)

Browallia speciosa

☼ ❖ ◌

Since this plant is propagated by seed, the season in which the blue-violet flowers appear depends on when the seeds were sown. The leaves are long and oval.

Min. winter temp. 10–15°C (50–59°F)
Ht. 75cm (30in); spr. 45cm (18in)

Brunnera macrophylla

Siberian bugloss

☀ ❖ ◌

A clump-forming perennial of the woodland edge that bears sprays of star-shaped blue flowers – resembling those of forget-me-nots – in early spring.

Ht. 45cm (18in); spr. 60cm (24in)

Campanula carpatica

Bellflower

☼ ☀ ☀ ❖ ◌

Good for use in drystone walls or shady urban gardens, this clump-forming rock perennial has long-lasting bell-shaped blue flowers in summer.

Ht. 8–10cm (3–4in); spr. 30cm (12in)
Also white

C. persicifolia

Bellflower

A woodland-edge perennial that bears bell-shaped flowers in summer. Its leaves are long and bright green.

Ht. 1m (3ft); spr. 30cm (12in)
Also white

Convolvulus sabatius

☼ ◇ ◌

In summer and early autumn this trailing perennial produces bright blue-purple bell-shaped flowers. Its stems are slim and bear small oval leaves.

Ht. 15–20cm (6–8in); spr. 30cm (12in)
Also white

Crocus 'Blue Pearl'

☼ ❖ ◌ ❋

There are many varieties of crocus (orange and white tend to be pecked by birds); this one bears lavender flowers in early spring.

Ht. and spr. 10cm (4in)

Cynara cardunculus

Cardoon

☼ ❖ ◌

In summer this open-ground perennial bears large blue-purple flowers that resemble thistles. A dramatic, sculptural species, it has grey pointed leaves.

Ht. 2m (6½ft); spr. 1m (3ft)

Delphinium belladonna 'Blue Bees'

☼ ❖ ◌

Ideal for cottage gardens, this bears spires of sky blue flowers in summer.

Ht. 1.5m (5ft); spr. 60cm (24in)
Also white

Dianella tasmanica

Flax lily

☼ ❖ ◌

This perennial is evergreen, with star-shaped blue-purple or bright blue summer flowers and deep blue autumn berries.

Ht. 1.2m (4ft); spr. 50cm (20in)

Digitalis purpurea

Foxglove

☼ ❖ ◌ ◌

In summer this woodland species bears tall spikes of purple flowers.

Ht. 1.5m (5ft); spr. 60cm (24in)
Also orange, white

Echinops ritro 'Veitch's Blue'

Globe thistle

☼ ❖ ◌ ✿

Round thistle-like late-summer flowers in shades of purple-blue characterise this upright perennial. Its stems are silver-grey.

Ht. 1.2m (4ft); spr. 75cm (30in)

Eryngium alpinum

Sea holly

☼ ❖ ◌

Although it bears purple-blue flower heads in summer, this open-ground species is often grown for its foliage, which is blue-grey and spiny.

Ht. 1m (3ft); spr. 60cm (24in)

E. x oliverianum

Sea holly

☼ ❖ ◌

In addition to its late-summer thistle-like lavender-coloured flowers, this has attractive grey-blue bracts (leaves at the

---

base of the flower head) and foliage.

Ht. 1m (3ft); spr. 60cm (24in)

Euphorbia characias subsp. wulfenii

Milkweed, spurge

☼ ❖ ◌

A species of most interest for its foliage, this evergreen bears clusters of grey-blue leaves and spikes of yellow-green flowers in spring.

Ht. 1.2m (4ft); spr. 1.3m (4½ft)

E. myrsinites

Milkweed, spurge

☼ ❖ ◌

A small evergreen rock plant with beautiful grey foliage.

Ht. 8cm (3in); spr. 25cm (10in)

Festuca glauca

Blue fescue

☼ ☀ ☀ ❖ ◌

Useful for its fine leaves, ranging from blue to silver in colour, this open-ground grass works very well in containers and naturalistic plantings.

Ht. and spr. 10cm (4in)

Helictotrichon sempervirens

Blue oat grass

☼ ❖ ◌

Grown for its stiff blue or silver leaves, this open-ground grass also bears spikes of oat-coloured flowers in summer.

Ht. 45cm (18in); spr. 60cm (24in)

Hyacinthoides

Bluebell

☼ ❖ ◌

A genus of several species of spring-

Helictotrichon sempervirens

flowering woodland plants all of which have blue flowers.

Ht. 30cm (12in); spr. 15cm (6in)

Iris germanica

☼ ☀ ❖ ◌

In late spring and early summer stems produce up to six violet-blue or purple-blue blooms, each up to 15cm (6in) across.

Ht. 1.2m (4ft); spr. 1m (3ft)
Also pink, yellow/orange, white

I. sibirica

☼ ☀ ❖ ◌

From late spring to early summer each stem bears two or three blue-purple or blue-veined blooms that are up to 10cm (4in) across.

Ht. 1.2m (4ft); spr. 1m (3ft)

Leymus arenarius

Lyme grass

☼ ☀ ☀ ❖ ◌

Grown for its foliage, this highly invasive perennial grass of open ground has broad steel blue leaves, and grey-green flowers in late summer.

Ht. to 1.5m (5ft); spr. indefinite

Iris germanica

Phlox divaricata
'Blue Dreams'

Liriope muscari
Lilyturf

☀ ❖ ❖ ◊

A woodland plant for autumn interest that produces spikes of clustered rounded lavender-coloured or blue-purple flowers late in the season, and has dark evergreen grass-like leaves.

Ht. 30cm (12in); spr. 45cm (18in)

Myosotidium hortensia
Chatham Island forget-me-not

☀ ❖ ◊ ◊

An evergreen with glossy mid-green ribbed leaves, this bears large clusters of small blue-mauve flowers in summer.

Ht. and spr. 60cm (24in)

Nepeta x faassenii
Catmint

☀ ❖ ◊

Flowering in early summer, this plant of sunny woodland edges works well in borders, producing spikes of blue-lavender flowers atop green-grey leaves. Loved by cats.

Ht. and spr. 45cm (18in)

Ruta graveolens
'Jackman's Blue'

Parochetus communis
☀ ❖ ◊

Brilliant blue flowers similar to those of a pea characterise this perennial blooming almost year round.

Ht. 5cm (2in); spr. 30cm (12in)

Phlox divaricata
☀ ❖ ❖ ◊

Ideal for rock gardens, this plant of the woodland edge has clusters of rounded blue-lavender flowers in early summer.

Ht. 30cm (12in); spr. 20cm (8in)

Polemonium caeruleum
Jacob's ladder

☀ ❖ ◊

A summer-flowering open-ground perennial with clusters of blue-lavender flowers.

Ht. and spr. 60cm (24in)

Ruta graveolens 'Jackman's Blue'
Rue

☀ ❖ ◊ ✳

Although this open species bears clusters of yellow flowers in summer, it is grown primarily for its evergreen blue foliage. Flowers must be removed to keep foliage attractive. May cause skin irritation.

Ht. and spr. 70cm (27in)

Salvia patens
Sage

☀ ❖ ◊

From late summer into autumn this perennial produces vibrant deep or pale blue flowers.

Ht. 60cm (24in); spr. 45cm (18in)

Scilla siberica 'Atrocoerulea'
Siberian squill

☀ ❖ ◊

An early-flowering woodland bulb with short spikes of bell-shaped blue flowers.

Ht. 15cm (6in); spr. 5cm (2in)

Streptocarpus saxorum
False African violet

☀ ◊ ◊

This evergreen with small hairy leaves has lilac-coloured flowers with white tubes in summer and autumn.

Min. winter temp. 10–15°C (50–59°F)
Ht. and spr. 35cm (14in)

Thalictrum aquilegiifolium
Meadow rue

☀ ❖ ◊

Purple-lilac summer flowers and fern-like green-grey leaves characterise this plant of the woodland edge.

Ht. 1.2m (4ft); spr. 45cm (18in)
Also white

Verbascum bombyciferum
Mullein

☀ ☀ ❖ ◊

Grown largely for its huge evergreen blue-grey oval leaves, which are covered in silver hairs, this also has yellow flowers in summer.

Ht. 2m (6½ft); spr. 60cm (24in)

Veronica gentianoides
☀ ❖ ◊

In early summer spikes of pale blue flowers top the glossy leaves of this rock plant.

Ht. and spr. 45cm (18in)

Ageratum houstonianum
Floss flower

☀ ❖ ◊

With their clusters of flowers in summer and autumn, these fast-growing plants are ideal for borders. Flower colour varies according to cultivar; some are sky blue, others lavender.

Ht. and spr. 30cm (12in)
Also pink, white

Campanula medium 'Bells of Holland'
Bellflower

☀ ❖ ◊

A slow-growing biennial ideal for cottage-style gardens. It has blue and lilac bell-shaped flowers in spring and summer.

Ht. 60cm (24in); spr. 30cm (12in)
Also pink, white

Centaurea cyanus
Bluebottle, cornflower

☀ ❖ ◊ ✿

Flowering through the summer into autumn, this fast-growing annual has brilliant blue daisy-like flowers.

Ht. 90cm (35in); spr. 30cm (12in)

Consolida
Larkspur

☀ ❖ ◊

Ideal for cottage gardens, these fast-growing annuals make lovely cut flowers.

Ht. 1.2m (4ft); spr. 30cm (12in)

Convolvulus tricolor
☀ ❖ ◊ ✿

This fast-growing upright annual has saucer-shaped blue flowers and green oval leaves.

Ht. 30cm (12in); spr. 20cm (8in)
Also white

Echium vulgare
☀ ❖ ◊

A fast-growing annual of open fields that bears spikes of blue and purple bell-shaped flowers. Its leaves are dark green.

Ht. 30cm (12in); spr. 20cm (8in)
Also pink, white

Felicia bergeriana
Kingfisher daisy

☀ ❖ ◊

Sun is necessary for this plant to open its small daisy-like blue flowers and reveal their yellow centres.

Ht. and spr. 15cm (6in)

Nemophila menziesii
Baby blue eyes

☀ ❖ ◊

This annual's blue flowers with white centres appear in summer, above green-grey leaves.

Ht. 20cm (8in); spr. 15cm (6in)

Nigella damascena 'Persian Jewels'
Love in a mist

☀ ❖ ◊

A fast-growing annual with flowers in various shades of blue in summer. Oval seed pods follow in autumn.

Ht. 45cm (18in); spr. 20cm (8in)
Also pink, white

Salvia sclarea var. turkestanica
Sage

☀ ❖ ◊ ✳

Clusters of somewhat strange-looking

Scilla siberica 'Atrocoerulea'

lavender flowers and lavender bracts (leaves at the base of the flower head) in summer characterise this open-ground annual. Its leaves are oval and aromatic.

Ht. 75cm (30in); spr. 30cm (12in)
Also white

Senecio maritima 'Silver Dust'
☀ ❖ ◊

An evergreen shrub grown as an annual for its silver-blue foliage. To keep the foliage silver, the daisy-like yellow summer flowers should be removed as they appear, although the white buds that precede them are very pretty.

Ht. and spr. 30cm (12in)

Viola 'Azure Blue'
Pansy

☀ ❖ ◊

Five-petalled spring flowers in pale blue-mauve with yellow centres characterise this bushy perennial usually grown as an annual. This is an archetypal cottage-garden plant.

Ht. and spr. 20cm (8in)

Salvia sclarea var. *turkestanica*

Magnolia x *soulangeana*

RED AND PINK

TREES, SHRUBS AND CLIMBERS

Abelia x grandiflora

☼ ❖ 🝌 🝆

Clusters of small pink and white tubular flowers cover this small evergreen in summer and autumn. Shelter from cool dry winds.

Ht. and spr. 3m (10ft)

Acer palmatum 'Atropurpureum'

Japanese maple

☼ ❖ 🝌

A deciduous small tree grown for its red-purple foliage, which turns bright red in autumn. Its spring flowers are small and red-purple. *A. p.* 'Dissectum Atropurpureum' has lovely lacy leaves, which turn brown and wretched with age.

Ht. and spr. 6m (20ft)

Acer palmatum 'Atropurpureum'

A. platanoides 'Crimson King'

Norway maple

☼ ❖ 🝌

A fast-growing tree planted for its foliage – deep red leaves, which are orange in autumn.

Ht. 20m (65ft); spr. 12m (40ft)

A. rubrum 'Schlesingeri'

Red maple

☼ ❖ 🝌

Autumn foliage is a rich deep red colour; during the rest of the year it is green. Its spring flowers are also red.

Ht. 20m (65ft); spr. 12m (40ft)

Actinidia kolomikta

☼ ❖ 🝌

A deciduous twining climber with attractive pale pink leaves, and white summer flowers.

Ht. 4m (13ft)

Albizia julibrissin

Silk tree

☼ ❖ 🝌

Clusters of pale pink flowers appear on this deciduous tree in late summer and autumn.

Ht. and spr. 10m (33ft)

Bauhinia variegata

☼ ❖ 🝌 ✳

This deciduous tree has dark red or pink flowers in winter and spring.

Min. winter temp. 15–18°C (59–64°F)
Ht. 8m (26ft); spr. 10m (33ft)

Berberis thunbergii f. atropurpurea

☼ ❖ 🝌

A dense shrub of most interest for its prickly red-purple foliage, which turns bright red in autumn.

Ht. 2.5m (8ft); spr. 3m (10ft)

Calliandra haematocephala

☼ ❖ 🝌

From late autumn through to spring this evergreen shrub bears pink flowers. Its leaves are narrow and green.

Min. winter temp. 7°C (45°F)
Ht. 2.5m (8ft); spr. 3m (10ft)
Also white

Callistemon rigidus

☼ ❖ 🝌

A bushy evergreen shrub with spikes of rich red flowers from late spring to early summer. Its leaves are dark green and pointed.

Ht. and spr. 2.5m (8ft)

Camellia

☼ ❖ 🝌 pH

A genus of evergreen shrubs, most of which can be trained against walls and are good in containers.

C. japonica 'Adolphe Audusson'

has deep red semi-double flowers and glossy leaves.

Ht. 10m (33ft); spr. 8m (26ft)

C. x williamsii 'Donation'

is upright and bears pink semi-double flowers.

Ht. 4m (13ft); spr. 2.5m (8ft)

Cercis canadensis

Eastern redbud

☼ ❖ 🝌

In spring the magenta buds of this spreading tree or shrub open to reveal pale pink flowers.

Ht. and spr. 10m (33ft)

Chaenomeles x superba

☼ ❖ 🝌

A bushy shrub with glossy dark green leaves and red flowers. Those of 'Knap Hill Scarlet' are salmon to scarlet; those of the free-flowering 'Rowallane' are crimson.

Ht. 1.5m (5ft); spr. 1.8m (6ft)

Cistus x purpureus

Rock rose

☼ ❖ 🝌

This evergreen shrub with green-grey foliage produces deep pink flowers with red flushes in early summer.

Ht. and spr. 1m (3ft)
Also white

Clianthus puniceus

Parrot's bill

☼ ❖ 🝌

Clusters of bright red flowers appear on this twining climber in spring and summer.

Ht. 3m (10ft)

Codiaeum variegatum

Croton

☼ ❖ 🝌

A leathery-leaved shrub grown for its foliage; leaves vary in size and are variegated with shades of orange, red, pink and yellow.

Min. winter temp. 10–13°C (50–55°F)
Ht. and spr. 1.2m (4ft)

Cordyline australis 'Atropurpurea'

☼ ❖ 🝌

Of most interest for its spiky red-purple leaves, this evergreen also bears white flowers in summer and white fruits in autumn. A sculptural species.

Min. winter temp. 5°C (41°F)
Ht. 10m (33ft); spr. 7m (23ft)

Cornus florida rubra

☼ ❖ 🝌

The bracts supporting the pale pink spring flowers of this deciduous spreading tree are pink or red.

Ht. and spr. 8m (26ft)

C. f. 'Welchii'

☼ ❖ 🝌

A deciduous spreading tree whose handsome green leaves are edged in pink and turn rich red-purple in autumn. Its small spring flowers are white.

Ht. and spr. 8m (26ft)

Cotinus coggygria 'Royal Purple'

Smoke tree

☼ ❖ 🝌

Dusky pink flowers and rich red-purple foliage characterise this deciduous shrub. It will tolerate shade, but the full colour of its foliage is only achieved in sunlight. It works well in plantings with pink or hot orange flowers.

Ht. and spr. 5m (16ft)

Daphne mezereum

☼ ❖ 🝌 ✳

Grown for its flowers and berries, this stiffly erect shrub produces deep pink flowers in early spring and red berries in summer. Its foliage is green-grey.

Ht. and spr. 1.2m (4ft)

Escallonia

☼ ❖ 🝌

A genus of evergreen shrubs, all of which have glossy green leaves and resist sea and salt winds well.

Also white

E. 'Donard Beauty'

bears deep pink flowers in early summer.

Ht. and spr. 1.5m (5ft)

E. 'Peach Blossom'

is rounded, with flowers of a rich peachy pink.

Ht. 1.8m (6ft); spr. 1.5m (5ft)

Euonymus alatus

Winged spindle

☼ ❖ 🝌

A dense shrub whose dark green leaves turn brilliant red in autumn.

Ht. 1.8m (6ft); spr. 3m (10ft)

Fagus sylvatica f. purpurea

Purple beech, copper beech

☼ ❖ 🝌

This plant's oval, ridged red-purple

Acer platanoides 'Crimson King'

Actinidia kolomikta

leaves turn a brilliant copper red in autumn.
Ht. 30m (100ft); spr. 25m (80ft)

Fuchsia 'Mrs Popple'
☀ ❈ ❖ ◊

An upright shrub with brilliant hanging red and purple flowers. Good for hedging if sheltered.
Ht. 1.5m (5ft); spr. 75cm (30in)

F. 'Versicolor'
☀ ❈ ❖ ◊

This has variegated creamy-green leaves and small red flowers.
Ht. 80cm (32in); spr. 1m (3ft)

Grevillea banksii
☀ ❖ ◊

An evergreen with slim green leaves and dense red flowers at intervals through the year. Can be grown in containers.
Min. winter temp. 10°C (50°F)
Ht. 6.5m (21ft); spr. 3m (10ft)

Hibiscus syriacus 'Woodbridge'
☀ ❖ ◊

This upright deciduous shrub bears large pink-red flowers with deeper centres in summer and autumn.
Ht. 2.5m (8ft); spr. 2m (6½ft)

Cotinus coggygria 'Royal Purple'

Ixora coccinea
☀ ❖ ◊

A small evergreen shrub producing clusters of small red and pink flowers in summer.
Min. winter temp. 13–16°C (55–61°F)
Ht. 1.2m (4ft); spr. 1.4m (4½ft)
Also yellow/orange

Justicia brandegeana
Shrimp plant
☀ ❖ ◊

An evergreen shrub that bears salmon pink flowers in summer and at intervals year round.
Min. winter temp. 10–15°C (50–59°F)
Ht. 1m (3ft); spr. 70cm (27in)

Kalmia latifolia
Mountain laurel, calico bush
☀ ❖ ◊ pH

This bushy evergreen shrub with glossy green foliage has clusters of pink summer flowers.
Ht. and spr. 3m (10ft)

Kolkwitzia amabilis
Beauty bush
☀ ❖

A deciduous arching shrub with masses of bell-shaped pink flowers in late spring and summer. Can be used for hedging.
Ht. and spr. 3m (10ft)

Lagerstroemia indica
☀ ❖ ◊

This deciduous tree bears sprays of pink and pink-mauve flowers in summer and autumn.
Ht. 7m (23ft); spr. 5m (16ft)

Lapageria rosea
Chilean bellflower
☀ ❖ ◊

A twining climber with long pink-red flowers in summer and autumn.
Ht. 5m (16ft)

Leptospermum scoparium 'Red Damask'
New Zealand tea tree, manuka
☀ ❖ ◊ ❈

In late spring and summer sprays of deep red flowers clothe this evergreen shrub. Its dark green leaves are narrow, giving a sparse, spiky effect.
Ht. and spr. 3m (10ft)

Leucospermum reflexum
☀ ❖ ◊

Usually grown for its flower heads, which in spring and summer bear slim deep red flowers, this evergreen shrub has grey foliage.
Min. winter temp. 10°C (50°F)
Ht. 3m (10ft); spr. 2.5m (8ft)

Magnolia campbellii
☀ ❖ ◊ ❈

Mature trees – over 15 years old – produce large pale pink flowers from winter into spring.
Ht. 20m (65ft); spr. 12m (40ft)

M. x soulangeana
☀ ❖ ◊ ❈

This spreading shrub or small tree bears large pink-tinged flowers in spring and early summer. The first flowers precede the spring foliage. This is a showy plant – one in your garden will always draw comments.
Ht. and spr. 6m (20ft)

Malus floribunda
Crab apple
☀ ❖ ◊

Red buds on this tree turn to a mass of pale pink blossom in spring, then form small currant-like fruits in autumn.
Ht. and spr. 3m (10ft)

M. 'John Downie'
Crab apple
☀ ❖ ◊

Following its white spring blossom, this tree produces edible orange-scarlet crab apples in autumn.
Ht. 10m (33ft); spr. 6m (20ft)

M. x purpurea
Purple crab
☀ ❖ ◊

A deciduous tree with red-tinged young leaves and deep red spring flowers, which pale with age. They are followed in autumn by reddish-purple round crab apples.
Ht. 8m (26ft); spr. 10m (33ft)

Mandevilla splendens
☀ ❖ ◊

A twining evergreen climber with shiny foliage, and red-pink flowers in late spring and summer.
Min. winter temp. 7–10°C (45–50°F)
Ht. 3m (10ft)

Metrosideros excelsa
Pohutukawa, New Zealand Christmas tree
☀ ❖ ◊

Dramatic and showy, this evergreen spreading tree bears large clusters of bright red flowers in winter.
Min. winter temp. 5°C (41°F)
Ht. 12m (40ft); spr. 13m (43ft)

Nandina domestica 'Firepower'
☀ ❖ ◊

Young specimens have red-tinged foliage year-round; in more mature specimens this colour is restricted to autumn. White summer flowers are followed in mild locations by red fruits.
Ht. 1.8m (6ft); spr. 1m (3ft)

Nerium oleander
Oleander
☀ ❖ ◊ ❈

From spring through to autumn, this evergreen shrub or small tree bears clusters of pink and red flowers on crimson stalks.
Min. winter temp. 10°C (50°F)
Ht. 4m (13ft); spr. 3m (10ft)

Parthenocissus quinquefolia
Virginia creeper, five-leaved ivy
☀ ❖ ◊

A self-clinging climber with purple berries and bright crimson foliage in autumn.
Ht. 15m (50ft)

P. tricuspidata 'Veitchii'
☀ ❖ ◊

A fast-growing self-clinging climber at its best in autumn when its leaves are vibrant red-purple.
Ht. 20m (65ft)

Phormium tenax 'Bronze Baby'
☀ ❖ ◊

This sculptural evergreen produces red flowers in summer, but is more often grown for its stiff pointed leaves which are claret coloured year-round.
Ht. and spr. 60cm (24in)

Photinia x fraseri 'Red Robin'
☀ ❖ ◊

Mature specimens of this evergreen shrub have glossy green leaves; young plants have bright red foliage. Cutting back promotes the growth of new red shoots and leaves.
Ht. 6m (20ft); spr. 4m (13ft)

Lapageria rosea

Pieris formosa var. forrestii
☀ ❖ ◊ pH

This evergreen shrub bears white flowers but is of most interest for its foliage – 'Wakehurst' has bright red leaves in spring, which turn through shades of pink and cream to green; the leaves of 'Variegata' are white variegated.
Ht. and spr. 3m (10ft)

Pimelea ferruginea
☀ ❖ ◊ pH

This evergreen bears clusters of bright pink flowers in spring and early summer.
Min. winter temp. 7°C (45°F)
Ht. 70cm (27in); spr. 1m (3ft)

Protea neriifolia
☀ ❖ ◊ pH

In spring and summer this evergreen shrub bears tall upright red or pink flower heads.
Min. winter temp. 5–7°C (41–45°F)
Ht. and spr. 3m (10ft)

Prunus 'Kanzan'
☀ ❖ ◊

Throughout spring this deciduous tree bears a profusion of large pink flowers.
Ht. and spr. 10m (33ft)

Malus floribunda

Rhododendron 'Barnstedt'

Pseudopanax ferox

☼ ❖ ◌

An evergreen tree with toothed green leaves with dusky red veins.
Ht. 5m (16ft); spr. 2.5m (8ft)

Quercus coccinea
Scarlet oak

☼ ❖ ◌

This species has leaves that are brilliant red for many weeks in autumn.
Ht. 25m (80ft); spr. 20m (65ft)

Rhaphiolepis indica
Indian hawthorn

☼ ❖ ◌ ❇

This evergreen bushy shrub has star-shaped pink flowers in spring and early summer, and dark glossy leaves.
Ht. 2m (6½ft); spr. 2.5m (8ft)

Rhododendron

☼ ❖ ◌ pH

This large genus of tree to dwarf deciduous and evergreen species, also

Telopea truncata

includes the azaleas.
Also blue/purple, white

R. 'Addy Wery' has vermilion flowers.
Ht. and spr. 1m (3ft)

R. 'Bagshot Ruby' has wide funnel-shaped bright ruby-red flowers.
Ht. 1.8m (6ft); spr. 1.5m (5ft)

R. 'Barnstedt' has fuschia pink flowers.
Ht. and spr. 1.5m (5ft)

R. 'Dreamland' has pale pink flowers with darker edges.
Ht. and spr. 1.2m (4ft)

R. 'Rosebud' bears rose pink flowers.
Ht. and spr. 1m (3ft)

Ribes sanguineum
Flowering currant

☼ ❖ ◌

A deciduous shrub bearing small pale or reddish pink flowers in spring. These are followed by black fruits.
Ht. and spr. 2m (6½ft)
Also white

Rosa
Rose

☼ ❖ ◌ ◌ ❇

A huge genus of many different kinds of

plants, often grown for their scented flowers. Sizes and cultivation details can vary enormously – be sure to get indications of both when you buy.
Also yellow/orange, white

R. 'New Dawn' is a climber, bearing clusters of pale shell pink blooms in summer and autumn.
Ht. and spr. 5m (16ft)

R. 'Roseraie de l'Haÿ' is a fragrant shrub bearing large deep crimson flowers in summer and autumn. Ideal for romantic gardens.
Ht. and spr. 2m (6½ft)

R. rugosa is a fast-growing species with large deep red flowers throughout summer and autumn, followed by large red hips.
Ht. and spr. 1.8m (6ft)

R. 'Souvenir du Docteur Jamain' is a hybrid bearing wine red scented flowers.
Ht. 1.8m (6ft); spr. 1m (3ft)

Spathodea campanulata
Flame of the forest, African tulip tree

☼ ❖ ◌

This bears clusters of bright red or orange-red flowers at intervals throughout the year. A showy specimen which always attracts attention.
Min. winter temp. 16–18°C (61–64°F)
Ht. 20m (65ft); spr. 13m (43ft)

Spiraea japonica

☼ ❖ ◌

A genus of small shrubs all of which bear heads of rose or crimson pink blooms in summer. Young specimens of

S. j. 'Anthony Waterer' also have brilliant red foliage which matures to dark green.
Ht. and spr. 1.2m (4ft)

Tamarix ramosissima

☼ ❖ ◌

This elegant deciduous shrub has small blue-green leaves and spikes of small pink flowers in summer and autumn.
Ht. 5m (16ft); spr. 4m (13ft)

Telopea truncata
Tasmanian waratah

☼ ❖ ◌ ❇ pH

A dense shrub bearing clusters of crimson flowers in spring and autumn.
Ht. 2.5m (8ft); spr. 3m (10ft)

Viburnum farreri

☼ ❖ ◌ ❇

This bears pale pink flowers in autumn and early spring and – in mild years or warmer areas – also in winter. In mature specimens foliage is dark green; younger plants have lighter leaves.
Ht. 3m (10ft); spr. 2.5m (8ft)

Weigela

☼ ❖ ◌

Deciduous shrubs grown for their funnel-shaped flowers.

W. 'Bristol Ruby' is a fast-growing shrub with deep red flowers in spring and summer.
Ht. 2.5m (8ft); spr. 1.8m (6ft)

W. florida 'Foliis Purpureis' has pale pink flowers and dark red leaves.
Ht. 1m (3ft); spr. 1.5m (5ft)

W. f. 'Variegata' has pink flowers and beautiful cream variegated foliage.
Ht. and spr. 1.5m (5ft)

PLANTS FOR DISPLAY AND GROUND COVER

Acaena microphylla

☼ ❖ ◌

An evergreen perennial of open dry grasslands that bears small flowers with spiny red bracts (leaves at the base of the flower clusters) in summer.
Ht. 5cm (2in); spr. 15cm (6in)

Achimenes 'Little Beauty'

☼ ❖ ◌

In summer this perennial produces large cone-shaped rich pink flowers with yellow centres.
Min. winter temp. 10°C (50°F)
Ht. 25cm (10in); spr. 30cm (12in)

Ajuga reptans 'Multicolor'

☼ ❖ ◌ ◌

This woodland-edge evergreen foliage plant has dark green leaves marked with cream and pink. It has small blue spikes of spring flowers.
Ht. 12cm (5in); spr. 45cm (18in)
Also red, green

Anemone x hybrida
Windflower

☼ ☼ ❖ ◌ ◌

A group of perennials, all with dark green leaves and attractive cup-shaped summer and autumn flowers. Originally plants of the woodland edge.

A. x h. 'Bressingham Glow' has deep pink flowers with yellow centres on wiry stems.
Ht. 1.5m (5ft); spr. 60cm (24in)

Dicentra eximia

A. x h. 'Max Vogel' has mauve-pink flowers on wiry stems.
Ht. 1.5m (5ft); spr. 60cm (24in)

A. x h. 'Prince Henry' has beautiful single deep pink blooms and slim stems.
Ht. 1.5m (5ft); spr. 60cm (24in)

Armeria maritima
Sea pink, thrift

☼ ❖ ◌ ◌

Dark green, narrow grass-like leaves and heads of masses of tiny pink-white summer flowers characterise this clump-forming perennial.
Ht. 10cm (4in); spr. 15cm (6in)
Also white

Asclepias syriaca
Silk weed

☼ ❖ ◌ ◌

In summer this upright perennial, originally a plant of dry grasslands, produces small pink-purple flowers on drooping stalks. When flowering is finished in early autumn, long pods filled with silky seeds appear, hence its common name.
Ht. and spr. 1.2m (4ft)

Filipendula rubra

Aster novae-angliae 'Alma Potschke'

A fast-growing perennial, originally from damp meadows, that bears clusters of dark pink flowers in autumn.

Ht. 75cm (30in); spr. 60cm (24in)

Astilbe

A genus of woodland plants bearing branched flower clusters and ferny leaves.

Also white

A. 'Bressingham Beauty' has small star-shaped vibrant pink flowers.

Ht. and spr. 1m (3ft)

A. 'Fanal' has pretty leaves and bright red summer flowers which keep their shape but turn brown in winter.

Ht. 60cm (24in); spr. 1m (3ft)

Caladium x hortulanum 'Pink Beauty'
Angels' wings

The large leaves of this perennial are mottled with pale pink and have dark pink veins.

Min. winter temp. 19°C (66°F)
Ht. and spr. 1m (3ft)

Chrysanthemum frutescens 'Mary Wootton'
Marguerite

Daisy-like pale pink flowers, blooming in summer, contrast with year-round dark green foliage. Originally a meadow plant.

Ht. and spr. 1m (3ft)
Also yellow, white

Colchicum autumnale
Autumn crocus, meadow saffron

A species of the woodland edge, this autumn-flowering corm bears pink or mauve-pink flowers.

Ht. and spr. 15cm (6in)
Also white

C. speciosum

One of a genus of corms that produce funnel-shaped flowers in spring or autumn. This species flowers in autumn.

Ht. and spr. 20cm (8in)

Cosmos atrosanguineus
Chocolate cosmos

Spikes of cherry red blooms appear on this perennial from mid to late summer; the leaves are tinged with copper red.

Ht. 1m (3ft); spr. 25cm (10in)

Dahlia 'Bishop of Llandaff'

With large deep red flowers in summer and autumn, this species can also be used as an ephemeral. Gives a rather dashing effect.

Ht. and spr. 1m (3ft)

Dianthus
Pink, carnation

A genus of mainly summer-flowering rock perennials, which make ideal borders for a cottage-garden path.

D. 'Gran's Favourite' has pale pink flowers with claret markings.

Ht. and spr. 30cm (12in)

D. 'Little Jock' has darker pink flowers, marked with claret.

Ht. and spr. 30cm (12in)

Dicentra eximia

In spring and summer small heart-shaped pink flowers hang from the arching branches of this woodland-edge perennial. Its foliage is green-grey and fern-like. A long-flowering plant, working well in mysterious gardens.

Ht. and spr. 30cm (12in)

Helleborus orientalis

D. spectabilis
Bleeding heart

In spring and summer heart-shaped rich pink flowers hang from the arching stems of this perennial. Leaves turn yellow when flowers have finished – but the plant is not dying.

Ht. 75cm (30in); spr. 50cm (20in)

Dierama pendulum
Angel's fishing rod

At the end of summer bell-shaped pink

flowers hang from the stems of this corm. A species of open ground.

Ht. 1.5m (5ft); spr. 20cm (8in)

Echinacea purpurea
Prairie coneflower

During summer this perennial of open ground bears daisy-like rich pink flowers with brown centres. Good in wildlife gardens or meadow lawns.

Ht. 1.2m (4ft); spr. 50cm (20in)

Erigeron 'Charity'

For most of the summer this pretty open-ground perennial bears masses of daisy-like pale pink flowers with yellow centres.

Ht. and spr. 60cm (24in)
Also blue

Eupatorium purpureum
Joe Pye weed

In late summer and early autumn, the heads of the stems of this upright open-ground

perennial bear pink flowers.

Ht. 2m (6½ft); spr. 1m (3ft)

Filipendula rubra

A plant that originated in damp meadows and is ideal for boggy sites, this perennial has beautiful leaves and produces small pink flowers on tall stems at the height of summer.

Ht. 2.5m (8ft); spr. 1.2m (4ft)

Geranium

Geraniums, originally plants of the woodland edge, are excellent ground-cover species.

Also blue

G. cinereum 'Ballerina' bears cup-shaped pink flowers with purple veins from late spring through the summer.

Ht. 10cm (4in); spr. 30cm (12in)

G. endressii 'Wargrave Pink' has bright pink flowers all summer long.

Ht. 45cm (18in); spr. 60cm (24in)

G. macrorrhizum is fragrant and grown primarily for its rich maroon-coloured flowers, which appear in early summer, but it also has attractive bright autumn leaves.

Ht. 38cm (15in); spr. 60cm (24in)

Geum 'Mrs Bradshaw'

Small sprays of scarlet flowers adorn this clump-forming woodland-edge perennial in summer.

Ht. 75cm (30in); spr. 45cm (18in)
Also yellow

Helleborus orientalis

In winter and early spring this dense woodland-edge evergreen bears cup-shaped pink flowers, sometimes spotted with deeper pinks. Ideal for mysterious gardens.

Ht. and spr. 45cm (18in)
Also white, purple

Heuchera x brizoides 'Coral Cloud'

A clump-forming perennial with green leaves and feathery sprays of pink flowers in summer.

Ht. 60cm (24in); spr. 45cm (18in)
Also purple, white

H. 'Palace Purple'

A rock perennial of most interest for its heart-shaped rich ruby red leaves.

Ht. and spr. 45cm (18in)

Liatris spicata
Gay feathers

A perennial with grass-like foliage. The upright stems of this open-meadow plant produce spikes of rose pink flowers in late summer.

Ht. 60cm (24in); spr. 30cm (12in)

Lotus berthelotii
Coral gem

The summer flowers of this perennial are bright red and similar to those of a pea; its foliage is silver grey. Good for hanging baskets and containers.

Min. winter temp. 5°C (41°F)
Ht. 30cm (12in); spr. 60cm (24in)

Paeonia officinalis 'Rubra Plena'

Monarda didyma 'Cambridge Scarlet'

☼ ❖ ◊ ❋

Masses of rich red flowers are borne in summer on this open-ground perennial.

Ht. 1m (3ft); spr. 45cm (18in)
Also purple, pink

Nertera granadensis
Bead plant

☼ ❖ ◊

This perennial is of most interest for the tiny scarlet berries that follow its white early-summer flowers. Needs to be watered well in summer so not a good choice for containers.

Ht. 12mm (½in); spr. 25cm (10in)

Paeonia officinalis 'Rubra Plena'
Paeony

☼ ❖ ◊

Luscious double red blooms with frilled

Paeonia 'Sarah Bernhardt'

petals characterise this beautiful species originally of the woodland edge. Frothy and ideal for romantic gardens.

Ht. and spr. 75cm (30in)
Also white

P. 'Sarah Bernhardt'
Paeony

☼ ❖ ◊ ❋

Large dusty pink blooms fading to white are the major feature of this perennial. A frothy and fragrant species, it is perfect for romantic gardens.

Ht. and spr. 1m (3ft)

Penstemon 'Apple Blossom'

☼ ❖ ◊

From midsummer onward this perennial bears sprays of small cone-shaped pale pink flowers.

Ht. and spr. 45cm (18in)
Also purple, red

Phlox paniculata 'Eva Callum'

☼ ❖ ◊

Bright pink flowers with deep red centres are borne in summer on this upright open-ground perennial. A

traditional cottage-garden classic.

Ht. 80cm (32in); spr. 50cm (20in)
Also purple, white

Polygonum bistorta 'Superbum'

☼ ❖ ◊

In summer this perennial ground cover of damp open meadows bears spikes of pale pink flowers.

Ht. 75cm (30in); spr. 60cm (24in)

Primula denticulata
Drumstick primula

☼ ☼ ❖ ◊ ❀

A fast-growing upright species of the woodland edge that bears pink or mauve flowers throughout the spring.

Ht. 30cm (12in); spr. 45cm (18in)
Also white

Pulmonaria rubra
Lungwort

☀ ❖ ◊ ◊

This woodland variety has rust-red blooms in winter and spring. An ideal ground cover.

Ht. 30cm (12in); spr. 60cm (24in)
Also blue, white

Russelia equisetiformis

☼ ❖ ◊

In summer and autumn this shrub bears clusters of vivid red flowers.

Min. winter temp. 15°C (59°F)
Ht. 1.1m (3½ft); spr. 60cm (24in)

Sedum spectabile 'Autumn Joy'
Ice plant

☼ ❖ ◊ ◊ ◊

The pink flowers of this plant turn bronze before dying; its leaves are grey and fleshy. A good species to dry.

Ht. and spr. 45cm (18in)

Tellima grandiflora 'Purpurea'
Fringecups

☼ ❖ ◊

This evergreen woodland species is of most interest for its foliage: it has masses of hairy deep red leaves. Its spring flowers are greenish.

Ht. and spr. 60cm (24in)
Also green

Viola labradorica 'Purpurea'

☼ ❖ ◊

The leaves of this perennial are tinged dark red. Good for shady rock gardens and wildlife gardens, this will also grow at the base of a hedge.

Ht. 5cm (2in); spr. 45cm (18in)

ANNUALS

Alcea rosea
Hollyhock

☼ ❖ ◊

In spring and summer upright spikes of large bright flowers in pink and red clothe this open-ground biennial. This is an ideal species for cottage gardens.

Ht. 1.8m (6ft); spr. 60cm (24in)
Also yellow, cream

Amaranthus caudatus
Love lies bleeding, tassel flower

☼ ❖ ◊

Long hanging tassels of deep red flowers in summer and autumn characterise this strange bushy annual.

Ht. 1.2m (4ft); spr. 45cm (18in)

Coleus blumei

☼ ❖ ◊

A fast-growing bushy perennial of most

interest for its bright, attractive leaves in shades of red and pink.

Min. winter temp. 10°C (50°F)
Ht. 45cm (18in); spr. 30cm (12in)

Dianthus barbatus
Sweet William

☼ ❖ ◊

In early summer broad flower heads carry several individual flowers, all two-coloured – white/pink, pale pink/cerise, red/magenta. Ideal for cottage gardens.

Ht. 45cm (18in); spr. 30cm (12in)

Impatiens Super Elfin series
Busy Lizzie

☼ ❖ ◊

Available in many shades, including red, pink and salmon.

Ht. 25cm (10in); spr. 45cm (18in)
Also white

Lavatera trimestris 'Silver Cup'

☼ ❖ ◊

A fast-growing annual clothed with cone-shaped pink flowers in summer and autumn.

Ht. 60cm (24in); spr. 45cm (18in)

Lunaria annua
Honesty

☼ ❖ ◊ ❋

Best known for its round silvery seed pods, this fast-growing woodland species also bears pink flowers in spring and summer.

Ht. 75cm (30in); spr. 30cm (12in)

Matthiola
Stock

☼ ❖ ◊ ❋

A large genus, with many varieties grown as

Amaranthus caudatus

annuals. Most annual varieties are scented – some at night – and ideal for cutting.

Ht. 75cm (30in); spr. 30cm (12in)
Also blue, white

Papaver somniferum
Opium poppy

☼ ❖ ◊

This fast-growing annual has large cup-shaped flowers in shades of red and pink, deepening to purple and paling to white.

Ht. 75cm (30in); spr. 30cm (12in)

Pelargonium Orbit series
Geranium

☼ ❖ ◊

Large round heads of dusky pink flowers in summer and autumn characterise this evergreen grown as an annual. Ideal for containers.

Ht. and spr. 60cm (24in)

Salvia splendens Cleopatra series

☼ ❖ ◊

In summer and early autumn this species bears clusters of bright red tubular flowers.

Ht. and spr. 30cm (12in)

Dianthus barbatus

Acer pseudoplatanus 'Brilliantissimum'

TREES, SHRUBS AND CLIMBERS

Acacia dealbata
Mimosa, silver wattle

☀ ❖ ◌ ✳

A fast-growing evergreen tree with fern-like lacy green-blue leaves, and bright yellow flower heads in winter and spring.
Ht. 12m (40ft); spr. 8m (26ft)

Acer cappadocicum 'Aureum'
Cappadocian maple

☀ ❖ ◌

The leaves of young specimens of this deciduous tree, most interesting for its foliage, are bright yellow in spring, turn pale green in summer and revert to yellow in autumn.
Ht. 20m (65ft); spr. 15m (50ft)

Acer cappadocicum 'Aureum'

A. pseudoplatanus 'Brilliantissimum'
Sycamore

☀ ❖ ◌ ✦

A slow-growing spreading tree that bears shrimp pink, then pale bronze, leaves.
Ht. and spr. 10m (33ft)

Campsis grandiflora
Chinese trumpet vine

☀ ❖ ◌

A self-clinging climber that produces trumpet-shaped warm orange flowers in late summer and autumn. Plants in warmer areas flower more prolifically.
Ht. 10m (33ft)

Cassia didymobotrya
Golden wonder

☀ ❖ ◌

This evergreen produces vibrant yellow flowers from its brown buds at intervals throughout the year.
Min. winter temp. 13°C (55°F)
Ht. 3m (10ft); spr. 2.5m (8ft)

Cupressus macrocarpa 'Goldcrest'
Monterey cypress

☀ ❖ ◌

Plumes of bright yellow foliage appear on this fast-growing conifer all year round.
Ht. 10m (33ft); spr. 5m (16ft)

Cytisus x kewensis
Broom

☀ ❖ ◌ ✦

This low arching shrub bears pale creamy lemon flowers in late spring.
Ht. 30cm (12in); spr. 1.5m (5ft)

C. x praecox
Warminster broom

☀ ❖ ◌ ✦

In spring this dense shrub produces masses of creamy lemon flowers, similar to those of a pea, among its tiny grey-green leaves.
Ht. 1m (3ft); spr. 1.5m (5ft)

Dendromecon rigida

☀ ❖ ◌ ✳

From spring to autumn this fast-growing shrub with green-grey foliage produces large golden flowers. It is ideal for training up a wall.
Ht. and spr. 3m (10ft)

Eccremocarpus scaber
Glory vine, Chilean glory flower

☀ ❖ ◌

This twining climber bears racemes of small orange flowers in summer. These are followed by seed pods containing winged seeds.
Ht. 3m (10ft)

Elaeagnus pungens 'Maculata'

☀ ❖ ◌ ✳ ✦

An evergreen shrub of most interest for its foliage – glossy yellow leaves, edged with dark green. Its short-lived inconspicuous autumn flowers are white.
Ht. 4m (13ft); spr. 5m (16ft)

Euonymus fortunei 'Emerald and Gold'

☀ ❖ ◌

This low-growing bushy evergreen shrub has green leaves edged with bright yellow all year round. Also good for ground cover.
Ht. 70cm (27in); spr. 1m (3ft)

Euryops pectinatus

☀ ❖ ◌

Bearing daisy-like bright yellow flowers in spring and early summer – and again sometimes in winter – this evergreen shrub also has green-grey leaves.
Min. winter temp. 5–7°C (41–45°F)
Ht. 1.2m (4ft); spr. 1m (3ft)

Forsythia

☀ ❖ ◌

A genus of deciduous shrubs, all of which bear their prolific bright yellow spring flowers before their leaves emerge. These are tough hardy plants. *F. x intermedia* 'Lynwood' is good for hedges.
Ht. 1.5m (5ft); spr. 2.5m (8ft)

Fremontodendron 'California Glory'

☀ ❖ ◌

From late summer to mid-autumn this evergreen shrub bears large vibrant yellow flowers; its leaves are round and dark green.
Ht. 6m (20ft); spr. 5.5m (18ft)

Genista aetnensis
Mount Etna broom

☀ ❖ ◌ ✳

This small rounded tree bears masses of golden flowers in midsummer. It casts very little shade.
Ht. 9m (33ft); spr. 10m (33ft)

G. lydia

☀ ❖ ◌

In spring and summer the arching branches of this deciduous shrub bear yellow flowers. It can grow over a low wall.
Ht. and spr. 60cm (24in)

Gleditsia triacanthos 'Sunburst'
Honey locust

☀ ❖ ◌

Bright golden foliage is the hallmark of this deciduous tree.
Ht. 13m (43ft); spr. 10m (33ft)

Hedera colchica 'Sulphur Heart'
Paddy's pride

☀ ❖ ◌

A self-clinging climber with variegated light green and yellow leaves. Needs sunlight to keep its leaves yellow.
Ht. 5m (16ft)

Hibbertia cuneiformis

☀ ❖ ◌

In spring and summer this bushy evergreen bears tiny clusters of vibrant yellow flowers.
Min. winter temp. 5–7°C (41–45°F)
Ht. 2.5m (8ft); spr. 1.5m (5ft)

Hypericum 'Hidcote'

☀ ❖ ◌

Large golden buttercup flowers appear on this

Fremontodendron 'California Glory'

round semi-evergreen shrub from midsummer through to autumn; its leaves are dark green. A very jolly plant.
Ht. 1.2m (4ft); spr. 1.5m (5ft)

Ilex aquifolium 'Golden Queen'
Holly

☀ ✳ ❖ ◌ ✦

The crinkled spiny evergreen leaves of this tree or large shrub have golden yellow edges.
Ht. 10m (33ft); spr. 6m (20ft)

Jasminum nudiflorum
Winter jasmine

☀ ❖ ◌

An arching shrub with dark green foliage and small bright yellow flowers in winter and spring. Grow against or tumbling over a wall.
Ht. and spr. 3m (10ft)

Lantana 'Spreading Sunset'

☀ ❖ ◌

Dense round flower heads bear small flowers in shades of orange from spring to autumn. This evergreen can be invasive in mild areas.
Min. winter temp. 10–13°C (50–55°F)
Ht. 1m (3ft); spr. 1.2m (4ft)

Hedera colchica 'Sulphur Heart'

Leonotis leonurus
Lion's ear

☼ ❖ ◗ ♨

This evergreen has vibrant orange flowers in autumn and winter.
Ht. 1.8m (6ft); spr. 1.5m (5ft)

Ligustrum ovalifolium 'Aureum'
Privet

☼ ❖ ◗ ♨ ❦

The glossy green leaves of this evergreen have bright yellow edges.
Ht. 4m (13ft); spr. 3m (10ft)

Lonicera japonica 'Halliana'
Japanese honeysuckle

☼ ❖ ◗ ❋ ❦

A twining climber with pale lemon flowers in summer and autumn.
Ht. 10m (33ft)

L. nitida 'Baggesen's Gold'
Honeysuckle

☼ ❖ ◗

This evergreen shrub has bright yellow leaves and yellow-green spring flowers. Cut back to keep leaves yellow.
Ht. 1.4m (4½ft); spr. 1.5m (5ft)

Mahonia x media 'Charity'

☼ ❖ ◗ ❋

Holly-like evergreen leaves and large spikes of yellow flowers from autumn to early spring characterise this shrub.
Ht. 4m (13ft); spr. 3m (10ft)

Sambucus racemosa 'Plumosa Aurea'

Pachystachys lutea
Lollipop plant

☼ ❖ ◗

This evergreen has bright yellow flowers in spring and summer.
Min. winter temp. 13–15°C (55–59°F)
Ht. 1.4m (4½ft); spr. 1.1m (3½ft)

Paeonia lutea ludlowii
Tree paeony

☼ ☼ ❖ ◗

Bearing bowl-shaped golden flowers in early summer, this has lovely bright green leaves.
Ht. and spr. 2.5m (8ft)

Philadelphus coronarius 'Aureus'
Mock orange

☼ ❖ ◗ ❋

An upright shrub with golden foliage in spring, green-yellow in summer. Its early summer cream flowers have an orange-blossom scent.
Ht. 2.5m (8ft); spr. 1.5m (5ft)
Also white

Potentilla

☼ ❖ ◗

A genus of deciduous shrubs bearing clusters of tiny rounded flowers, like those of wild roses.
Also red/pink, white

P. 'Elizabeth' has primrose yellow flowers from midsummer on.
Ht. 90cm (35in); spr. 1.2m (4ft)

P. fruticosa is dense and bushy with bright yellow or orange flowers all summer.
Ht. 1m (3ft); spr. 1.5m (5ft)
Also white

Robinia pseudoacacia 'Frisia'
False acacia

☼ ❖ ◗

A deciduous tree of most interest for its

fine yellow foliage which turns orange-yellow in autumn.
Ht. 15m (50ft); spr. 7.5m (25ft)

Sambucus racemosa 'Plumosa Aurea'
Red-berried elder

☼ ❖ ◗ ❦

A beautiful deciduous shrub with yellow leaves when young, golden when mature. Keep pruning to maintain the yellow. Striking against a green shady bed.
Ht. and spr. 3m (10ft)

Sorbus 'Joseph Rock'
Mountain ash

☼ ❖ ◗ ❦

An upright tree of most interest for its clusters of small bright yellow berries in late summer and autumn, and for its pretty leaves.
Ht.10m (33ft); spr. 7.5m (25ft)

Tecoma stans
Yellow elder

☼ ❖ ◗

From spring and into autumn cone-shaped yellow flowers adorn this evergreen tree.
Min. winter temp. 13°C (55°F)
Ht. 5.5m (18ft); spr. 4m (13ft)

Thuja occidentalis 'Rheingold'

☼ ☼ ❖ ◗

A slow-growing conifer whose foliage is golden from spring to autumn and bronze in winter.
Ht. and spr. 4m (13ft)

Thunbergia alata
Black-eyed Susan

☼ ❖ ◗

In summer and autumn this twining annual climber has orange-yellow flowers with dark "eyes" at the centre.
Ht. 3m (10ft)

PLANTS FOR DISPLAY AND GROUND COVER

Achillea 'Coronation Gold'

☼ ❖ ◗ ❦

A perennial with large flat golden flower heads in summer. Ideal for cottage gardens.
Ht. 1m (3ft); spr. 60cm (24in)

A. 'Moonshine'

☼ ❖ ◗

Vibrant yellow flower heads and grey foliage characterise this plant all summer.
Ht. 60cm (24in); spr. 50cm (20in)

Aphelandra squarrosa 'Louisae'
Zebra plant

☼ ❖ ◗

An evergreen with long glossy leaves deeply veined with white. Bright yellow flower heads appear in late summer and autumn.
Min. winter temp. 13°C (55°F)
Ht. 1m (3ft); spr. 60cm (24in)

Carex elata 'Aurea'
Bowles golden sedge

☼ ❖ ◗

An evergreen woodland grass grown for its golden yellow foliage; its summer flower spikes are brown.
Ht. 40cm (16in); spr. 15cm (6in)

Eremurus stenophyllus
Foxtail, king's spear

☼ ❖ ◗

An open-ground species with strap-like leaves, and curving spikes of bright yellow flowers in summer. It needs rich porous soil that dries out in summer.
Ht. 1m (3ft); spr. 60cm (24in)

Euphorbia polychroma
Milkweed, spurge

☼ ❖ ◗

A bushy perennial with bright yellow flowers for most of the spring.
Ht. and spr. 50cm (20in)
Also blue

Filipendula ulmaria 'Aurea'

☼ ❖ ◗

Of most interest for its fern-like yellow spring foliage, in midsummer this perennial of damp meadows has clusters of cream flowers.
Ht. and spr. 30cm (12in)

Gaillardia pulchella
Blanket flower

☼ ❖ ◗

A fast-growing species with grey-green leaves and bright yellow daisy-like flowers.
Ht. 45cm (18in); spr. 30cm (12in)
Also red/pink

Helenium 'Moerheim Beauty'
Sneezeweed

☼ ❖ ◗ ❦

Sprays of daisy-like velvety orange-bronze flowers appear in early

Achillea 'Coronation Gold'

autumn on this upright open-ground species.
Ht. 1m (3ft); spr. 60cm (24in)

Helianthemum 'Jubilee'
Rock rose

☼ ❖ ◗

An evergreen rock plant that has saucer-shaped lemon flowers from spring to autumn. *H. 'Henfield Brilliant'* has burnt orange flowers.
Ht. 25cm (10in); spr. 30cm (12in)
Also red/pink, white

Hemerocallis
Daylily

☼ ❖ ◗ ❋

A genus of perennials of the woodland edge. Each flower lasts only a day, over some weeks.
Also red/pink

H. 'Golden Chimes' has small golden flowers and strap-like leaves.
Ht. 75cm (30in); spr. 60cm (24in)

Carex elata 'Aurea'

Lilium 'Enchantment'

H. lilio–asphodelus bears bright yellow flowers and has strap-like leaves.
Ht. and spr. 75cm (30in)

H. 'Stella d'Oro' has bell-shaped pale orange flowers from summer to the first frosts.
Ht. and spr. 45cm (18in)

Kniphofia 'Royal Standard'
Red-hot poker

☼ ❖ ◗

The flower spikes of this perennial bear scarlet buds, which open from bottom to top to reveal brilliant yellow flowers. Foliage is grass-like.
Ht. 1.2m (4ft); spr. 60cm (24in)
Also red

Lilium
Lily

☼ ❖ ◗ ❋

A genus of summer-flowering bulbs grown for their bright flowers.
Also white, pink

L. 'Enchantment' has orange-red flowers in early summer.
Ht. 1m (3ft); spr. 30cm (12in)

L. henryi produces its bright orange flowers in late summer.
Ht. 3m (10ft); spr. 30cm (12in)

Eremurus stenophyllus

L. lancifolium (tiger lily) flowers in summer and early autumn and has orange-red flowers; one type has yellow flowers.
Ht. 1.5m (5ft); spr. 30cm (12in)

Narcissus
Daffodil

☼ ◑ ❖ ◗

A genus of bulbs that flower in spring and early summer. The flowers consist of flat petals and a trumpet-shaped cup.

N. poeticus is fragrant and has small yellow or orange cups and yellow petals.
Ht. 40cm (16in); spr. 15cm (6in)

N. 'Tête-à-tête' has deep yellow cups and slightly paler petals.
Ht. 30cm (12in); spr. 10cm (4in)

Origanum vulgare 'Aureum'
Wild marjoram

☼ ❖ ◗ ◖ ❋

Of most interest for its dense mats of golden spring leaves, this herb from open woodland edges has small reddish flowers in late summer.
Ht. 8cm (3in); spr. 1m (3ft)

Primula

☼ ◑ ❖ ◗ ◖

A large genus of woodland-edge plants, some of which are evergreen, to suit almost any site or style of garden.

P. bulleyana is upright and bears deep orange flowers in early summer.
Ht. 60cm (24in); spr. 30cm (12in)

P. vulgaris (primrose) is a spreading species with pale lemon flowers.
Ht. and spr. 20cm (8in)

Rudbeckia hirta
Coneflower

☼ ❖ ◗

A fast-growing perennial of open ground, its brilliant yellow or orange daisy-like flowers last through summer and autumn.
Ht. 1m (3ft); spr. 40cm (16in)

Solidago 'Laurin'
Goldenrod

☼ ❖ ◗ ❧

This open-ground perennial has green foliage and bears spikes of rich yellow flowers in late summer. It is invasive, however, and can cause hayfever.
Ht. 75cm (30in); spr. 45cm (18in)

Strelitzia reginae
Bird-of-paradise flower

◑ ✕ ◗

A clump-forming perennial with green-blue leaves. It bears dramatic spiky orange and blue flowers in red bracts (leaves at the base of the flower head) in spring.
Min. winter temp. 5–10°C (41–50°F)
Ht. 1m (3ft); spr. 75cm (30in)

Trollius europaeus
Globeflower

☼ ❖ ◗

The rounded spring flowers of this clump-forming perennial of damp meadows are buttercup yellow.
Ht. 60cm (24in); spr. 45cm (18in)

Waldsteinia ternata

☼ ❖ ◗

The late spring and summer flowers of this woodland perennial are yellow; it forms mats of ground cover.
Ht. 10cm (4in); spr. 30cm (12in)

ANNUALS

Antirrhinum majus
Snapdragon

☼ ❖ ◗

Flowering from spring to autumn, these perennials are often grown as annuals. They are tall and branching, with lipped flowers in warm shades of orange, yellow and bronze. There is a wide variety of cultivars; good for cottage gardens.
Ht. 1m (3ft); spr. 45cm (18in)
Also purple, red/pink, white

Calceolaria 'Sunshine'

☼ ❖ ◗

Heads of small golden flowers appear from late spring to summer.
Ht. and spr. 20cm (8in)

Calendula officinalis
Pot marigold

☼ ❖ ◗ ❋

There are tall and dwarf varieties of this fast-growing annual, all of which flower from spring to autumn.
Ht. and spr. 60cm (24in)

Cheiranthus cheiri 'Fire King'
Wallflower

☼ ❖ ◗ ❋

In spring four-petalled flowers bloom in shades of lemon through bronze to orange. Tall, medium and dwarf cultivars exist; good for cottage and wildlife gardens.
Ht. 60cm (24in); spr. 40cm (16in)
Also red, white

Eschscholzia californica

☼ ❖ ◗

A fast-growing annual with cup-shaped flowers that bloom from summer to the end of autumn. Flowers vary from creamy lemon

through bronze to vibrant orange. Good for wildlife gardens.
Ht. 30cm (12in); spr. 15cm (6in)

Gazania uniflora

☼ ❖ ◗

This long-flowering species bears grey leaves and orange or yellow daisy-like flowers. Can be used as ground cover in frost-free areas in winter.
Ht. 23cm (9in); spr. 30cm (12in)

Glaucium flavum
Horned poppy

☼ ❖ ◗ ·

This plant bears poppy-like bright yellow flowers in summer and early autumn, but is not a true poppy.
Ht. 60cm (24in); spr. 45cm (18in)

Helianthus annuus
Sunflower

☼ ❖ ◗

In summer this fast-growing annual bears large daisy-shaped flower heads. Good for cottage and wildlife gardens.
Ht. 3m (10ft); spr. 45cm (18in)

Antirrhinum majus

Limnanthes douglasii
Meadow foam

☼ ❖ ◗ ❋

Creamy flowers with bright yellow centres bloom all summer on this fast-growing species.
Ht. 15cm (6in); spr. 10cm (4in)

Tagetes erecta
African marigold

☼ ❖ ◗ ❋

A fast-growing species with glossy leaves and large daisy-like flowers in summer and autumn. Tall, intermediate and dwarf varieties exist.
Ht. 1m (3ft); spr. 45cm (18in)

T. patula
French marigold

☼ ❖ ◗ ❋

In summer and autumn this fast-growing species has yellow, orange or russet-coloured flowers. There are several varieties, all small.
Ht. and spr. 30cm (12in)

Glaucium flavum

Prunus 'Tai Haku'

WHITE AND CREAM
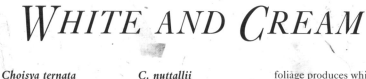

Gardenia jasminoides

TREES, SHRUBS AND CLIMBERS

Acer negundo 'Variegatum'
Box elder, ash-leaved maple

When they first open, the green leaves of this fast-growing deciduous spreading tree are tinged with pink; later in the summer they are edged with white. In spring insignificant greeny-yellow flowers appear.
Ht. 15m (50ft); spr. 13m (43ft)

Betula utilis var. jacquemontii
West Himalayan birch

Both bark and branches of this tree are brilliant white. It casts light shade.
Ht. 15m (50ft); spr. 7.5m (25ft)

Brugmansia x candida
Angels' trumpet

In summer and autumn white or cream bell-shaped flowers hang from this tree. Its leaves are poisonous.
Min. winter temp. 10°C (50°F)
Ht. and spr. 4m (13ft)

Choisya ternata
Mexican orange blossom

This round evergreen shrub has beautiful glossy green leaves; its early summer flowers are white and fragrant.
Ht. and spr. 2.7m (9ft)

Clethra alnifolia
Sweet pepper bush

pH

This bushy deciduous shrub bears spires of small bell-shaped flowers in summer and early autumn. Its oval leaves are bright green.
Ht. and spr. 2.5m (8ft)

Cornus alba 'Elegantissima'
Red-barked dogwood

Of year-round interest, this fast-growing deciduous shrub has white-edged leaves in spring and summer, small cream-coloured summer flowers, white autumn fruits and red shoots in winter.
Ht. and spr. 2m (6½ft)

C. florida
Flowering dogwood

A deciduous tree bearing white or pink-white bracts (leaves at the base of the flower heads) in spring. The flowers are insignificant, but the bright green leaves turn purple in autumn.
Ht. 6m (20ft); spr. 8m (26ft)

C. nuttallii
Pacific dogwood, mountain dogwood

A deciduous tree with oval dark green leaves that bears tiny white flowers and large white bracts (leaves at the base of the flower heads) toward the end of spring.
Ht. 14m (46ft); spr. 10m (33ft)

Drimys winteri
Winter's bark

A conical-shaped evergreen with long glossy dark green leaves; its summer flowers are fragrant, white and star shaped.
Ht. 15m (50ft); spr. 10m (33ft)

Eucryphia x nymansensis

An elegant evergreen tree with glossy leaves that bears clusters of large white flowers in summer and early autumn.
Ht. 15m (50ft); spr. 7.5m (25ft)

Gardenia jasminoides
Cape jasmine, common gardenia

pH

From summer to winter this slow-growing elegant evergreen bears double white flowers.
Min. winter temp. 15°C (59°F)
Ht. and spr. 1.5m (5ft)

Hebe albicans

This dense evergreen shrub with blue-grey foliage produces white flowers in summer.
Ht. 60cm (24in); spr. 1m (3ft)

Hedera canariensis 'Gloire de Marengo'
Canary Island ivy

Ideal for growing up or trailing over a wall, this fast-growing evergreen self-clinging climber has large grey-green leaves with white margins. Severe frost may damage this species, but it will recover.
Ht. 6m (20ft)

Hoheria lyallii

At the height of summer this spreading tree produces clusters of white flowers. Its foliage is grey-green.
Ht. and spr. 7.5m (25ft)

Hoya australis

Clusters of up to 50 star-shaped flowers, usually tinged with crimson, appear on this twining climber in summer.
Min. winter temp. 15°C (59°F)
Ht. 5m (16ft)

Hydrangea macrophylla 'Mme E. Mouillère'

From mid to late summer this shrub bears domed heads of white flowers tinged with pink. A very showy species, this is also excellent in romantic gardens.
Ht. 1m (3ft); spr. 1.5m (5ft)
Also blue, red

Ilex aquifolium 'Argentea Marginata Pendula'
Perry's weeping silver holly

Ideal for small gardens, this shrub or small tree is grown for its dark green leaves which are fringed with creamy white.
Ht. 6m (20ft); spr. 5m (16ft)

Jasminum officinale
Common jasmine

A twining climber that bears clusters of small white flowers in summer and autumn.
Ht. 12m (40ft)

Magnolia grandiflora
Bull bay

At intervals from midsummer to early autumn this evergreen with big glossy green leaves bears large white flowers. A grand species.
Ht. and spr. 10m (33ft)

Michelia figo

This evergreen's glossy green leaves make a beautiful contrast with

Betula utilis var. *jacquemontii*

Rhamnus alaternus 'Argenteovariegata'

its cream flowers in spring and summer.

Min. winter temp. 5°C (41°F)
Ht. and spr. 5m (16ft)

Myrtus communis
Common myrtle

☼ ❖ ◌ ❋

In spring and summer this bushy shrub has aromatic dark green leaves and white flowers.

Ht. 2m (6½ft); spr. 2.5m (8ft)

Paulownia tomentosa
Foxglove tree, princess tree

☼ ❖ ◌ ❋

The fragrant sprays of the white-pink flowers of this spreading tree resemble foxgloves.

Ht. 15m (50ft); spr. 12m (40ft)

Philadelphus 'Virginal'

☼ ❖ ◌ ❋

This fast-growing deciduous shrub bears a profusion of large, highly scented white flowers in summer.

Ht. 3m (10ft); spr. 2.5m (8ft)

Pittosporum eugenioides 'Variegatum'

☼ ❖ ◌

The margins of the dark glossy leaves of this evergreen are white.

Ht. 9m (33ft); spr. 5m (16ft)

P. 'Garnettii'

☼ ☼ ❖ ◌

An evergreen that is of most interest for its foliage – its grey-green leaves are fringed with white. A pretty species.

Ht. 4m (13ft); spr. 3m (10ft)

Prunus 'Tai Haku'
Great white cherry

☼ ❖ ◌

In mid-spring this fast-growing spreading tree

---

bears single large brilliant white flowers.

Ht. 8m (26ft); spr. 10m (33ft)

Pyrus salicifolia 'Pendula'

☼ ❖ ◌

This small weeping tree has grey-white foliage and bears white flowers in spring.

Ht. and spr. 8m (26ft)

Rhamnus alaternus 'Argenteovariegata'
Italian buckthorn

☼ ☼ ❖ ◌

The glossy leaves of this evergreen shrub are edged with cream.

Ht. and spr. 3m (10ft)

Rhaphiolepis umbellata

☼ ❖ ◌ ❋

Clusters of white flowers appear on this evergreen in early summer.

Ht. and spr. 1.5m (5ft)

Rubus 'Benenden'

☼ ❖ ◌

In spring and summer this arching shrub bears large white flowers, which look like single wild roses.

Ht. and spr. 3m (10ft)

Sorbaria aitchisonii

☼ ☼ ❖ ◌ ◌

This arching shrub bears upright plumes of star-shaped flowers.

Ht. and spr. 3m (10ft)

Spiraea 'Arguta'
Foam of May, bridal wreath

☼ ❖ ◌

From the middle of spring into summer this dense shrub bears clusters of five-petalled white flowers. Ideal for mysterious gardens.

Ht. and spr. 2.5m (8ft)

Cimicifuga racemosa

S. nipponica 'Snowmound'

☼ ❖ ◌

A deciduous shrub with arching branches that bear clusters of small white summer flowers.

Ht. and spr. 2.5m (8ft)

Syzygium paniculatum
Australian brush cherry

☼ ❖ ◌ ❋

This evergreen tree with glossy leaves bears creamy white flowers in spring and summer and purple fruits in autumn.

Min. winter temp. 10°C (50°F)
Ht. 13m (43ft); spr. 7.5m (25ft)

Westringia fruticosa
Rosemary

☼ ❖ ◌

The spring and summer flowers of this shrub are white, often tinged with blue.

Min. winter temp. 5–7°C (41–45°F)
Ht. and spr. 1.5m (5ft)

Yucca gloriosa
Spanish dagger

☼ ❖ ◌

This evergreen has long stems of bell-shaped white flowers in summer and autumn and year-round spiky leaves.

Ht. 2m (6½ft); spr. 2.5m (8ft)

PLANTS FOR DISPLAY AND GROUND COVER

Arabis caucasica

☼ ❖ ◌ ❋

In late spring and summer this rock evergreen bears white flowers. It can be used in drystone walls.

Ht. 15cm (6in); spr. 25cm (10in)
Also pink

Aruncus dioicus
Goat's beard

☼ ❖ ◌

Large summer plumes of small creamy white flowers and large fern-like divided leaves characterise this woodland perennial.

Ht. 2m (6½ft); spr. 1.2m (4ft)

Arundo donax 'Versicolor'
Giant reed

☼ ❖ ◌

A large perennial grass of open ground near rivers. It has powerful stems of elegantly drooping cream-striped leaves.

Ht. 3m (10ft); spr. 60cm (24in)

Astrantia major
Masterwort

☼ ☼ ❖ ◌

A woodland species that bears delicate white flowers tinged with pink. Ideal for mysterious gardens.

Ht. 60cm (24in); spr. 45cm (18in)

Chrysanthemum x superbum
Shasta daisy

☼ ❖ ◌

This species of open sunny meadows bears single large daisy-like flowers in summer.

Good for cottage gardens.

Ht. 1m (3ft); spr. 60cm (24in)

Cimicifuga racemosa
Bugbane

☼ ❖ ◌

At the height of summer this clump-forming woodland perennial bears fine spikes of feathery brilliant white flowers; its leaves are ferny.

Ht. 1.5m (5ft); spr. 60cm (24in)

Convallaria
Lily-of-the-valley

☼ ❖ ◌ ❋

A genus of rhizomes of the woodland edge that bear short spikes of small bell-shaped flowers in spring.

Ht. 25cm (10in); spr. 60cm (24in)

Cortaderia selloana 'Silver Comet'
Pampas grass

☼ ❖ ◌

This open-ground evergreen grass has silvery white leaves and may also bear feathery white plumes in summer.

Ht. 1.5m (5ft); spr. 1m (3ft)

Crambe cordifolia

☼ ❖ ◌ ❋

Huge dense clouds of tiny flowers, rather like gypsophila, appear on the branching stems of this vigorous perennial in summer. Good for romantic gardens and creating a sense of space.

Ht. 2m (6½ft); spr. 1.2m (4ft)

Dieffenbachia 'Exotica'
Leopard lily, dumb cane

☼ ❖ ◌

The leaves of this evergreen are heavily

Crambe cordifolia

Hosta crispula

marked with splashes of creamy white.

Min. winter temp. 15°C (59°F)
Ht. and spr. 1.2m (4ft)

Galanthus nivalis
Common snowdrop

☀ ❖ 💧 🌙

Often the first bulb to break ground in winter, this plant bears tiny hanging flowers into early spring. A good species for growing under trees.

Ht. 15cm (6in); spr. 8cm (3in)

Gypsophila paniculata 'Bristol Fairy'

☀ ❖ 💧

Throughout the summer this perennial bears tiny, double white flowers on wiry branching stems. Its leaves are dark green.

Ht. 75cm (30in); spr. 1m (3ft)

Hesperis matronalis
Sweet rocket, dame's violet

☀ ❖ 💧 🌙 ❄

At their most fragrant in the evening, the white flowers of this upright perennial are borne on long spikes.

Ht. 75cm (30in); spr. 60cm (24in)

Hosta crispula

☀ ❖ 💧 💧

Heavily ridged green leaves edged with white characterise this attractive woodland foliage plant. Ideal for planting around the edge of a pond.

Ht. and spr. 1m (3ft)

H. fortunei 'Aurea Marginata'

☀ ❖ 💧 💧

Both the leaf edges and parts of the leaves of this species bear creamy white splashes.

Ht. and spr. 1m (3ft)

Iberis sempervirens
Candytuft

☀ ❖ 💧

A rock evergreen with dense white flowers in late spring and summer. Ideal in rock gardens.

Ht. 30cm (12in); spr. 60cm (24in)

Lamium maculatum 'Beacon Silver'
Deadnettle

☀ ☀ ❖ 💧 💧

Native to the woodland edge, this species is of most interest for its silver-white often mauve tinged oval leaves, but it also produces pink flowers. Excellent for ground cover.

Ht. 20cm (8in); spr. 1m (3ft)

Miscanthus sinensis 'Zebrinus'

☀ ❖ 💧

This grass has tall arching leaves with crosswise white and cream markings. A species that originated in open ground.

Ht. 1.2m (4ft); spr. 45cm (18in)

Pachysandra terminalis

☀ ❖ 💧

Smooth dark green leaves on this woodland evergreen are offset by tiny white flowers in early summer. An excellent ground-cover species for moist sites.

Ht. 10cm (4in); spr. 20cm (8in)

Papaver orientale 'Perry's White'
Oriental poppy

☀ ❖ 💧 🌙

Strong stems support the beautiful silky creamy white summer flowers with deep purple centres of this open-ground perennial. Plants may need staking as they grow to prevent blooms from drooping.

Ht. 80cm (32in); spr. 60cm (24in)
Also red/pink, orange

Papaver orientale 'Perry's White'

Plectranthus coleoides 'Variegatus'

☀ ❖ 💧 🌙

The scalloped edges of this evergreen's green-grey leaves are white.

Min. winter temp. 10°C (50°F)
Ht. and spr. 75cm (30in)

Polygonatum x hybridum
Solomon's seal

☀ ❖ 💧

In spring white tubular flowers hang from the arching branches of this woodland rhizome.

Ht. 1.2m (4ft); spr. 1m (3ft)

Pulmonaria 'Sissinghurst White'
Lungwort

☀ ❖ 💧

This has white spring flowers and leaves splashed with white.

Ht. 30cm (12in); spr. 60cm (24in)
Also red

Romneya coulteri
Californian poppy

☀ ❖ 💧 ❄

Large white flowers with bright yellow centres and grey foliage characterise this open-ground perennial. Can be invasive.

Ht. and spr. 2m (6½ft)

Saxifraga x urbium
London pride

☀ ❖ 💧

This woodland evergreen bears tiny white star-shaped flowers in summer.

Ht. 30cm (12in); spr. 60cm (24in)

Sisyrinchium striatum

☀ ❖ 💧

A semi-evergreen with tall and narrow handsome grey-green leaves. Spikes of cream-coloured flowers appear all summer long.

Ht. 60cm (24in); spr. 45cm (18in)

Smilacina racemosa
False spikenard

☀ ❖ 💧 pH

The arching pale green leaves of this woodland perennial bear spikes of cloudy white flowers from spring through to the height of summer.

Ht. 1m (3ft); spr. 45cm (18in)

Thymus x citriodorus 'Silver Queen'
Thyme

☀ ❖ 💧 🌙

A rock species with silvery white foliage.

Ht. 10cm (4in); spr. 25cm (10in)

Veronica virginica f. alba

☀ ❖ 💧

In late summer this upright open-ground perennial bears tall spikes of tiny star-shaped white flowers.

Ht. 1.2m (4ft); spr. 45cm (18in)

Vinca major 'Variegata'
Greater periwinkle

☀ ❖ 💧

A spreading woodland evergreen with small glossy leaves edged with creamy white. A good ground-cover species.

Ht. 45cm (18in); spr. 1.5m (5ft)

Zantedeschia aethiopica
Arum lily

☀ ❖ 💧

Tall elegant stems produce beautiful white flowers in summer.

Ht. 1m (3ft); spr. 60cm (24in)

ANNUALS

Dimorphotheca pluvialis
Rain daisy

☀ ❖ 💧

The summer flowers of this branching annual are small, white and daisy-like.

Ht. 30cm (12in); spr. 15cm (6in)

Lobularia maritima
Sweet alyssum

☀ ❖ 💧 ❄

A genus of small fast-growing annuals that bear tiny white honey-scented flower heads through summer and autumn. Ideal for wildlife gardens.

Ht. 15cm (6in); spr. 30cm (12in)
Also pink

Nicotiana alata

☀ ☀ ❖ 💧

In summer this perennial grown as an annual forms clusters of white flowers. Fragrant at night.

Ht. 75cm (30in); spr. 30cm (12in)
Also red/pink

Petunia x hybrida

☀ ❖ 💧

Fast-growing perennial grown as an annual. There are many varieties, all of which have attractive flowers of different sizes and shapes, some double and some striped.

Ht. and spr. 30cm (12in)
Also blue/purple, red/pink

Vinca major 'Variegata'

Helleborus foetidus, p.65

GREEN AND GREY

TREES, SHRUBS AND CLIMBERS

Buxus sempervirens
Common box, English boxwood
☼ ☀ ❖ ◗ ◗
Good for hedges and screens, this evergreen has glossy, dark green oblong leaves.
Ht. and spr. 5m (16ft)

Cedrus deodara
Deodar
☼ ☀ ❖ ◗
A conifer with grey-green needle-like foliage and a drooping habit.
Ht. 25m (80ft); spr. 10m (33ft)

C. libani
Cedar of Lebanon
☼ ❖ ◗
A conifer with branches of flat dark grey-green foliage. Magnificent when mature.
Ht. 25m (80ft); spr. 20m (65ft)

Chamaerops humilis

Chamaerops humilis
Dwarf fan palm
☼ ❖ ◗
An evergreen palm bearing several spikes of elongated leaves from a single trunk.
Ht. and spr. 1.5m (5ft)

Coprosma repens
☼ ❖ ◗
This evergreen has oval shiny green leaves; female plants bear red berries in autumn.
Min. winter temp. 2°C (36°F)
Ht. and spr. 1.8m (6ft)

Cotoneaster 'Cornubia'
☼ ❖ ◗
A semi-evergreen shrub or small tree with dark green foliage. White flowers appear in summer and hanging bunches of large scarlet fruits in autumn.
Ht. and spr. 6m (20ft)

C. lacteus
☼ ❖ ◗
Dark green oval leaves, white summer flowers and scarlet autumn fruits characterise this evergreen shrub. Ideal for hedges or screens.
Ht. 5m (16ft); spr. 4m (13ft)

Cryptomeria japonica
Japanese cedar
☼ ☀ ❖ ◗
A fast growing conifer with reddish bark and dark green leaves.
Ht. 20m (65ft); spr. 8m (26ft)

Cyathea australis
Australian rough tree fern
☼ ❖ ◗
A fern with a long black trunk and pale green fronds. Mysterious.
Min. winter temp. 13°C (55°F)
Ht. 8m (26ft); spr. 5m (16ft)

Dracaena draco
Dragon tree
☼ ❖ ◗
An evergreen with stiff grey-green leaves and bright orange berries.
Min. winter temp. 13°C (55°F)
Ht. and spr. 9m (33ft)

Elaeagnus x ebbingei
☼ ❖ ◗ 🍂
Insignificant but fragrant silver flowers set off the silvery foliage of this evergreen in autumn.
Ht. and spr. 5m (16ft)

Fatsia japonica
Japanese aralia
☼ ☀ ❖ ◗
This round evergreen shrub has large exotic-looking glossy dark green leaves; clusters of white flowers bloom in autumn. A good structural plant.
Ht. and spr. 3m (10ft)

Feijoa sellowiana
Pineapple guava
☼ ❖ ◗
A dense shrub with dark green leaves year-round, large crimson summer flowers and edible fruits in autumn.
Ht. and spr. 3m (10ft)

Garrya elliptica
Silk-tassel bush
☼ ❖ ◗
In winter into spring this evergreen shrub bears grey-green catkins; its leaves are leathery and dark green.
Ht. and spr. 5.5m (18ft)

Ginkgo biloba
Maidenhair tree
☀ ● ❖ ◗
Fan-shaped green leaves and edible fruits in autumn characterise this deciduous conifer.
Ht. 30m (100ft); spr. 10m (33ft)

Griselinia littoralis
Broadleaf
☼ ❖ ◗
This evergreen has apple green laurel-like leaves. Good for coastal gardens and hedges.
Ht. 6m (20ft); spr. 5m (16ft)

Hamamelis mollis
Chinese witch hazel
☼ ☀ ❖ ◗
In spring and summer this deciduous shrub has glossy leaves, which in autumn turn bronze.
Ht. and spr. 4.5m (15ft)

Hebe pinguifolia 'Pagei'
Disk-leaved hebe
☼ ❖ ◗
An evergreen spreading shrub with rounded grey leaves, ideal for rock or gravel gardens. Its flowers are white.
Ht. 30cm (12in); spr. 1m (3ft)

H. rakaiensis
☼ ❖ ◗
An evergreen shrub with grass green leaves; neat, like box, this can be used for hedging.
Ht. 1m (3ft); spr. 1.2m (4ft)

Hedera colchica
Persian ivy
☼ ● ❖ ◗
A fast-growing self-clinging climber ideal for growing up walls; its oval leaves are dark green.
Ht. 10m (33ft)

H. helix
Common English ivy
☼ ● ❖ ◗
This fast-growing self-clinging climber with dark green leaves can be trained up or over a wall.
Ht. 10m (33ft)

Itea ilicifolia
☼ ❖ ◗
A bushy shrub bearing catkins of pale green flowers in summer and autumn and glossy dark green leaves all year. Good against a wall.
Ht. and spr. 3m (10ft)

Juniperus scopulorum 'Skyrocket'
Rocky Mountain juniper
☼ ☀ ❖ ◗
An upright dwarf conifer with grey-blue foliage and blue berries.
Ht. 8m (26ft); spr. 75cm (30in)

J. virginiana 'Grey Owl'
Pencil cedar
☼ ☀ ❖ ◗
A low spreading conifer with silver-grey foliage.
Ht. 3m (10ft); spr. 5m (16ft)

Koelreuteria paniculata
Pride of India
☼ ❖ ◗
A deciduous tree with grass green leaves in spring and summer, bronze ones in autumn.
Ht. and spr. 10m (33ft)

Laurus nobilis
Sweet bay, bay laurel
☼ ☀ ❖ ◗ 🍂 ✳
An evergreen with dark glossy leaves, pale yellow spring flowers followed by clusters of green, then black fruits.
Ht. 12m (40ft); spr. 10m (33ft)

Leycesteria formosa
Himalayan honeysuckle
☼ ❖ ◗
This upright shrub has blue-green shoots and dark green leaves on bamboo-like stems. A strange-looking species.
Ht. and spr. 1.8m (6ft)

Liriodendron tulipifera
Tulip tree
☼ ❖ ◗ 🍂
The dark green leaves of this fast-growing deciduous tree turn bronze in autumn. At the height of summer it bears white flowers tinged with green.
Ht. 30m (100ft); spr. 20m (65ft)

Lonicera pileata
Honeysuckle
☀ ❖ ◗
This low spreading dense evergreen has

Cryptomeria japonica

Juniperus virginiana
'Grey Owl'

narrow shiny dark green leaves. A contrasting shrub sets it off well.
Ht. 70cm (27in); spr. 2.5m (8ft)

Macadamia integrifolia
Macadamia nut

This evergreen's leaves are mid-green and glossy; in spring it bears upright clusters of small creamy white flowers.
Min. winter temp. 10–13°C (50–55°F)
Ht. 15m (50ft); spr. 20m (65ft)

Nothofagus dombeyi

A conical evergreen with glossy dark leaves that droop at the tips.
Ht. 20m (65ft); spr. 10m (33ft)

Olearia macrodonta

This fast-growing evergreen has shiny grey leaves with silvery-white undersides and white daisy-like flowers in summer.
Ht. 6m (20ft); spr. 5m (16ft)

Osmanthus delavayi

An evergreen shrub with small glossy leaves

Olearia macrodonta

---

that bears small white flowers for a few weeks in spring. Smart looking.
Ht. and spr. 4m (13ft)

Pernettya 'Mother of Pearl'

A spreading evergreen shrub that needs male and female for berries.
Ht. and spr. 1m (3ft)

Phlomis fruticosa
Jerusalem sage

This evergreen has upright shoots and grey-green leaves. Its flowers are mustard yellow.
Ht. and spr. 1m (3ft)

Pittosporum tenuifolium

An evergreen with glossy oval grass green leaves with crinkly edges.
Ht. 6m (20ft); spr. 4.5m (15ft)

Podocarpus salignus

A conifer with long glossy leaves and reddish peeling bark.
Ht. 12m (40ft); spr. 7.5m (25ft)

Populus nigra 'Italica'
Lombardy poplar

A deciduous tree with bright green leaves and, in spring, red catkins. Keep away from drains and buildings.
Ht. 30m (100ft); spr. 5m (16ft)

Prunus laurocerasus 'Zabeliana'
Cherry laurel

This dense evergreen has narrow glossy dark green leaves; its white spring flowers are followed by cherry-like fruits in summer.
Ht. 1.2m (4ft); spr. 2.5m (8ft)

P. lusitanica
Portugal laurel

A bushy evergreen shrub that bears dark glossy oval leaves on dark red stems. Spikes of white spring flowers are followed by purple fruits in summer.
Ht. and spr. 10m (33ft)

Pseudopanax crassifolius
Lancewood

An evergreen with long narrow spiky leaves when plants mature. Female trees bear fruits.
Ht. 6m (20ft); spr. 1.8m (6ft)

Pyracantha 'Mohave'
Firethorn

A bushy evergreen with white flowers in early summer and orange fruits in autumn.
Ht. 4m (13ft); spr. 5m (16ft)

Rhapis excelsa
Bamboo palm, slender lady palm

Long glossy green leaves characterise this fanning palm.
Min. winter temp. 15°C (59°F)
Ht. and spr. 2.5m (8ft)

Rhus typhina
Staghorn sumach

A spreading deciduous tree or shrub with dark green fern-like leaves that turn copper in autumn, and dark red fruits held upright.
Ht. and spr. 6m (20ft)

Santolina chamaecyparissus
Cotton lavender

This dense evergreen shrub has sticky narrow

---

grey-white leaves, and shoots covered with fluffy white growth.
Ht. 75cm (30in); spr. 1m (3ft)

Sarcococca confusa
Christmas or sweet box

A dense evergreen with small glossy leaves.
Ht. and spr. 1m (3ft)

Schefflera actinophylla
Queensland umbrella tree

An upright evergreen with large attractive dark leaves.
Min. winter temp. 16°C (61°F)
Ht. 12m (40ft); spr. 11m (36ft)

Senecio laxifolius 'Dunedin Sunshine'

An evergreen shrub with oval pale-grey leaves, and yellow daisy-like flowers in summer.
Ht. 1m (3ft); spr. 2m (6½ft)

Sinarundinaria nitida

This evergreen bamboo has small pointed bright green leaves. Stems are often purple.
Ht. 5m (16ft); spr. 3m (10ft)

Skimmia japonica 'Rubella'

An evergreen shrub with dark green leaves. White flowers are followed by red fruits if male and female plants are grown together.
Ht. and spr. 1.5m (5ft)

Symphoricarpos x chenaultii 'Hancock'

A deciduous shrub with bronze leaves when young, bright green when mature. Good for wildlife gardens.
Ht. 1m (3ft); spr. 3m (10ft)

Taxodium distichum
Bald or swamp cypress

A deciduous tree ideal for wet sites. Its bright green leaves turn orange-brown at the end of autumn.
Ht. 22.5m (74ft); spr. 11m (36ft)

Teucrium fruticans
Shrubby germander

Grey leaves with white undersides characterise this arching evergreen shrub, which has bright blue summer flowers.
Ht. 1.8m (6ft); spr. 4m (13ft)

Thamnocalamus spathaceus
Muriel bamboo

A hollow-stemmed evergreen bamboo with long bright green leaves.
Ht. 4m (13ft); spr. 2m (6½ft)

Thujopsis dolobrata
Hiba

The glossy green leaves of this bushy conifer have silver undersides. It has grey cones.
Ht. 20m (65ft); spr. 10m (33ft)

Trachycarpus fortunei
Windmill palm

The tall trunk of this evergreen palm is topped with a large head of fan-like grass green leaves. Sprays of lemon flowers appear in early summer.
Ht. 12m (40ft); spr. 5m (16ft)

Viburnum davidii

A rounded evergreen shrub with deeply veined dark green leaves and, in spring, small heads of white flowers.

Phlomis fruticosa

Does not like wind, which burns its leaves.
Ht. 1.2m (4ft); spr. 1.5m (5ft)

V. tinus
Laurustinus

A bushy evergreen shrub that has oval dark green leaves and, from the end of winter to spring, heads of small white flowers. It will grow in shade, but only flowers if grown in sun.
Ht. and spr. 3m (10ft)

Vitis coignetiae
Crimson glory vine

The large veined leaves of this fast-growing deciduous twining climber are green in spring and summer, russet in autumn.
Ht. 15m (50ft)

Washingtonia robusta
Thread palm

A fast-growing evergreen palm with large fan-shaped green leaves above a tall slim trunk; its summer flowers are cream and winter berries black.
Min. winter temp. 10°C (50°F)
Ht. 15m (50ft); spr. 6m (20ft)

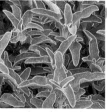

Pittosporum tenuifolium

Viburnum davidii

PLANTS FOR DISPLAY AND GROUND COVER

Acanthus spinosus

☼ ◈ ◊

Also of interest for its mauve summer flowers, this rock and scree perennial bears tall spikes of arching glossy green leaves. Menacing and sinister.

Ht. 1.2m (4ft); spr. 1m (3ft)

Aciphylla aurea
Golden Spaniard

☼ ◈ ◊

An evergreen perennial with long spiky vicious golden green leaves.

Ht. and spr. 75cm (30in)

Alchemilla mollis
Lady's mantle

◑ ◈ ◊

An excellent woodland-edge ground-cover species with pale green leaves and, in summer, sprays of tiny yellow-green flowers which last for ages in water.

Ht. and spr. 50cm (20in)

Artemisia
Wormwood

☼ ◈ ◈ ◊ ✳

A genus of perennials and spreading shrubs, originating in dry rocky

Ophiopogon planiscapus

areas, usually grown for their beautiful aromatic silver foliage. 'Powis Castle' is particularly attractive.

Ht. 1m (3ft); spr. 1.2m (4ft)

Bergenia 'Bressingham White'

☼ ◑ ◈ ◊

Good evergreen ground cover, this woodland-edge species has bold rounded leaves and white spring flowers.

Ht. and spr. 30cm (12in)

Calathea zebrina
Zebra plant

✸ ◈ ◊

An evergreen with velvety leaves; ribs and veins are pale green, the rest is dark green.

Min. winter temp. 15°C (59°F)
Ht. and spr. 1m (3ft)

Chamaemelum nobile 'Treneague'
Camomile

☼ ◈ ◊

This is the less invasive variety of camomile, a species of open ground. It can be used for lawns, but does not smell as good as the original variety. Can be threadbare.

Ht. 10cm (4in); spr. 45cm (18in)

Cyperus involucratus

✸ ◈ ◊

An evergreen with tufts of long thin leaves, which in summer support white flowers.

Min. winter temp. 4–7°C (39–45°F)
Ht. 1m (3ft); spr. 30cm (12in)

Epimedium x rubrum

◑ ◈ ◊

A woodland species with heart-shaped green leaves. Remove old foliage before it flowers.

Ht. 30cm (12in); spr. 20cm (8in)

Gladiolus 'Green Woodpecker'

☼ ◈ ◊

This bears green flowers with burgundy throats in summer.

Ht. 1.5m (5ft); spr. 30cm (12in)

Gunnera manicata

☼ ◈ ◊

This perennial with huge prickle-edged leaves needs space and a stretch of water to do it justice. A sinister plant.

Ht. and spr. 2.2m (7ft)

Helleborus foetidus
Stinking hellebore

◑ ◈ ◊

An evergreen of the woodland edge with deeply divided dark green leaves and, in winter and spring, pale green flowers which last for months.

Ht. and spr. 45cm (18in)

H. lividus subsp. corsicus

☼ ◈ ◊

A perennial evergreen with dark green leaves and cup-shaped light green flowers.

Ht. 60cm (24in); spr. 45cm (18in)

Liriope spicata

☼ ◈ ◊

An excellent ground-cover species, this evergreen has glossy, dark green grass-like leaves.

Ht. and spr. 40cm (16in)

Macleaya cordata
Plume poppy

☼ ◈ ◊

This spreading open-ground perennial has blue-grey leaves, and plumes of whitish flowers in summer. Very invasive.

Ht. 1.8m (6ft); spr. 75cm (30in)

Maranta leuconeura
Prayer plant

◑ ◈ ◊

A branching evergreen with velvety dark green leaves with white veins.

Min. winter temp. 15°C (59°F)
Ht. and spr. 30cm (12in)

Ophiopogon planiscapus 'Nigrescens'

◑ ◈ ◊

An extraordinary black-leaved grass-like woodland perennial. It forms low slow-spreading clumps and has short spikes of lilac flowers in summer.

Ht. and spr. 30cm (12in)

Osmunda regalis
Royal fern

◑ ◈ ◊

A rather grand deciduous woodland fern with bright green fronds. Mature plants bear tassels of non-descript russet flowers.

Ht. 1.8m (6ft); spr. 1m (3ft)

Phyllitis scolopendrium

☼ ◑ ◈ ◊

A genus of evergreen woodland ferns with tall, slightly arching, leathery bright green leaves.

Ht. 75cm (30in); spr. 45cm (18in)

Polystichum setiferum
Soft shield fern

◑ ◈ ◊

An evergreen with long arching spreading leaves.

Ht. 60cm (24in); spr. 45cm (18in)

Raoulia australis

☼ ◈ ◊

A creeping evergreen perennial, the leaves of which form a dense grey mat. Good for rock and stone gardens.

Ht. 12mm (½in); spr. 30cm (12in)

Rheum palmatum
Ornamental rhubarb

✳ ◈ ◊ ◊

An open-ground perennial with deep-cut rounded and lobed mid-green leaves and large frothy cream flowers.

Ht. and spr. 1.8m (6ft)

Rodgersia aesculifolia

☼ ◈ ◊

A woodland species, good for wildlife and water gardens, this perennial has crinkled yellow-green leaves.

Ht. and spr. 1m (3ft)

Stachys byzantina 'Silver Carpet'

☼ ◈ ◊

The furry grey leaves of this evergreen form a dense mat. Good for rock and stone gardens.

Ht. 15cm (6in); spr. 60cm (24in)

Stipa gigantea
Golden oats

☼ ◈ ◊

This perennial grass of open ground bears tufts of silvery-green in summer. A good feature on its own in a bed.

Ht. 2.5m (8ft); spr. 1m (3ft)

Symphytum grandiflorum
Comfrey

☼ ◑ ◈ ◊

An excellent ground cover, this woodland plant has long thin hairy vibrant green leaves.

Ht. 25cm (10in); spr. 60cm (24in)

Verbascum bombyciferum
Mullein

☼ ◑ ◈ ◊

This evergreen has oval grey leaves covered in tiny silver hairs. A sculptural species.

Ht. 1.8m (6ft); spr. 60cm (24in)

Stipa gigantea

ANNUALS

Kochia scoparia f. trichophylla
Burning bush

☼ ◈ ◊

Narrow bright green leaves characterise this fast-growing annual.

Ht. 90cm (35in); spr. 60cm (24in)

Moluccella laevis
Bells of Ireland

☼ ◈ ◊

A fast-growing annual with rounded green leaves and, in summer, spikes of white flowers with pale green calyxes.

Ht. 60cm (24in); spr. 20cm (8in)

Nicotiana alata 'Lime Green'
Tobacco plant

☼ ◈ ◊ ✳

Mid-green leaves and green flowers in summer and autumn characterise this perennial grown as an annual.

Ht. 60cm (24in); spr. 30cm (12in)

Zinnia 'Envy'

☼ ◈ ◊

This fast-growing annual has large daisy-like green flowers in summer and autumn and pale green leaves.

Ht. 60cm (24in); spr. 30cm (12in)

Verbascum bombyciferum

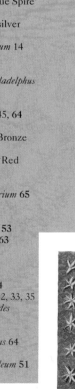

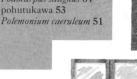

*A*CKNOWLEDGMENTS

t = top *c* = centre *b* = bottom *l* = left *r* = right

PICTURE CREDITS
Camera Press: 13*r*, 47. Andrew Crace: 31*br*. Derek Fell's Horticultural Picture
Library: 8*t*, 12*l*, 23*bl*, 23*br*, 27*bl*, 28*bl*, 44*t*. The Garden Picture Library: John Ainsworth
54*bl*; David Askham 61*t*; Clive Boursnell 14*bcl*, 54*br*; Lynne Brotchie 44*b*; Linda Burgess
57*br*, 59*tr*; Rex Butcher 11*bcl*, 29*bl*; Brian Carter 11*bcr*, 14*r*, 22*r*, 57*bl*, 59*bl*, 63*bl*–63*br*,
65*bl*–65*tr*; Bob Challinor 48*tl*, 49*r*; Henk Dijkman 38*br*; David England 55*b*, 64*br*; Ron
Evans 56*bl*, 60*bl*; Christopher Fairweather 39*br*, 51*tl*, 51*br*, 62*t*, 64*bl*; Vaughan Fleming
53*tr*; John Glover *cover*; 3*b*, 5*br*, 12*c*, 10*bc*, 39*t*, 43*tr*, 48*tr*, 50*t*, 51*bl*, 52*t*–52*bl*, 53*br*, 54*tr*, 57*tr*,
59*tl*, 60*tr*, 64*tl*, 64*tr*; Gil Hanly 15*t*; Sunniva Harte 55*t*; Marijke Heuff 6*t*, 7, 16*br*–17, 43*br*;
Neil Holmes 9*br*, 15*br*, 38*t*, 58*tr*; Roger Hyam 42*tl*, 56*tr*; Lamontagne 11*bc*, 53*tl*, 56*b*;
Mayer/Le Scanff 3*t*, 42*c*, 50*br*; John Miller 33*c*; John Neubauer
13*c*; Clive Nichols 33*t*, 51*tr*, 63*t*; Jerry Pavia 65*br*; Joanne Pavia
46*t*, 50*tr*–50*bl*, 65*tl*; Howard Rice 14*bl*, 15*bc*, 41, 43*bl*, 60*tl*; Gary
Rogers 9*bcr*, 38*bl*, 40*b*, 42*b*, 48*br*; David Secombe 27*tr*; J.S. Sira
5*bl*, 10*bl*, 12*r*, 49*c*, 54*tl*, 58*br*, 59*br*; Ron Sutherland 31*bl*, 32*l*, 39*bl*,
45, 52*br*; Brigitte Thomas 2; Juliette Wade 42*tr*, 61*b*; Didier
Willery 40, 42*tc*, 43*tl*, 48*bl*–48*bl*, 49*b*, 53*bl*, 56*tl*, 58*bl*, 60*br*, 62*c*–62*b*;
Steven Wooster 5*bc*, 11*t*, 26*bcl*, 46*b*. Haddonstone Ltd., East

Haddon, Northampton: 30*br*. Robert Harding Picture Library: 4–5*t*, 14*t*, 29*tlc*. HLD
Ltd.: 28*br*. Andrew Lawson: 32–33. Roland Lewis: 26*tl*. Marshalls Mono Ltd.: 21*bl*.
Outdoor Lighting (OLS): Hugh Palmer 33*b*. Harry Smith Collection: 6*c*, 8*bl*–8*br*,
9*bl*–9*bc*, 10*br*, 11*bl*, 11*br*, 12*cl*, 13*l*–13*cb*, 15*bc*–14*bcr*, 15*bl*. Stapley Water Gardens Ltd.:
30*tl*, 30*bl*. Whichford Pottery: 10*t*. Woodgiangrande: 23*tl*; Hugh Palmer 9*t*; Dominic
Turner 24–25; Julie Phipps 28*b*. Zooid Pictures: 5*tc* , 6*b*, 16,
20–21, 22–23, 26–27, 28–29, 30*tr*, 31*t*, 32*r*. Zooid Pictures wishes
to acknowledge Camden Garden Centre, Capital Gardens,
Fulham Palace Garden Centre.

ARTWORK CREDITS
David Ashby: 7*bl*, 18–19*c*, 34–35*c*, 34–35*bl*. Gary Cross: 6*br*, 34*cl*.
Katherine Harkness: 3*tl*, 6*cl*, 8–15 (groundplans), 48–65 (symbols).
Lorraine Harrison: 70–72. Coral Mula: 33*bl*. Kate Osborne:
32*ct*, 33*tl*, 33*tr*. Liz Pepperell: 33*bc*. Sandra Pond: 32*bl*.
Nadine Wickenden: 1*t*, 1*bc*, 7*tl*, 7*bl*, 66–68 (corners), stickers

40–676–01

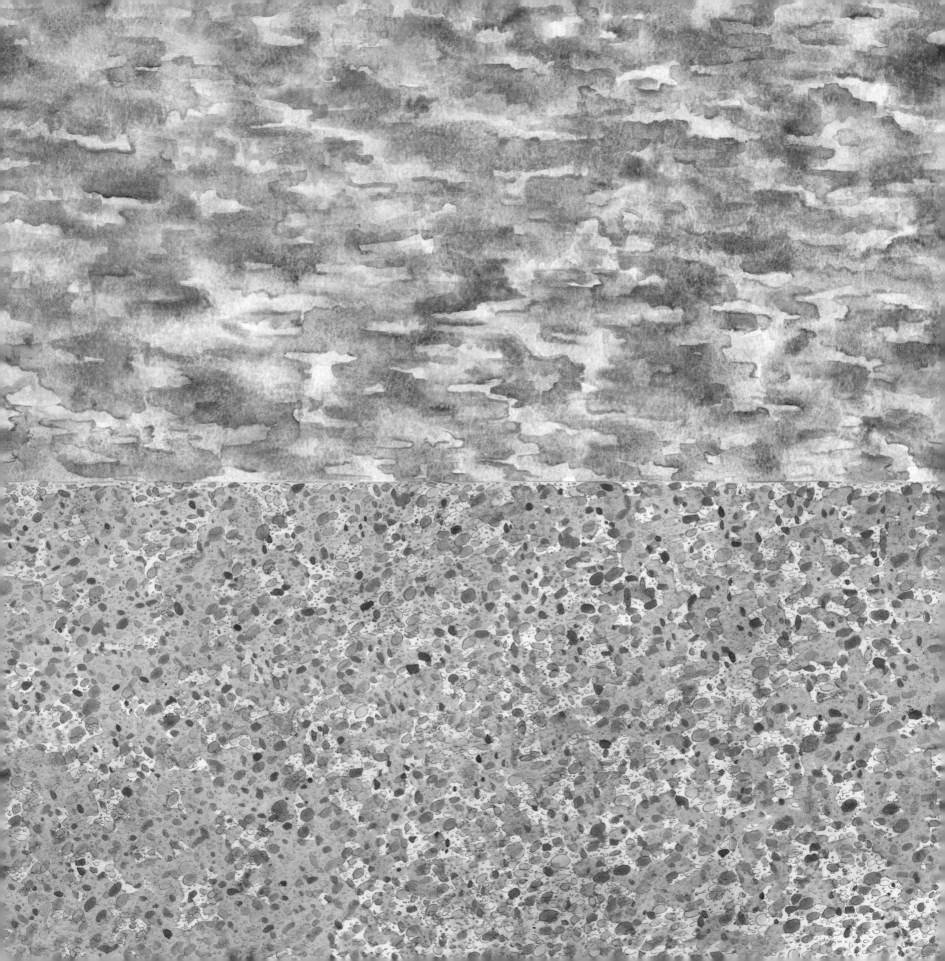

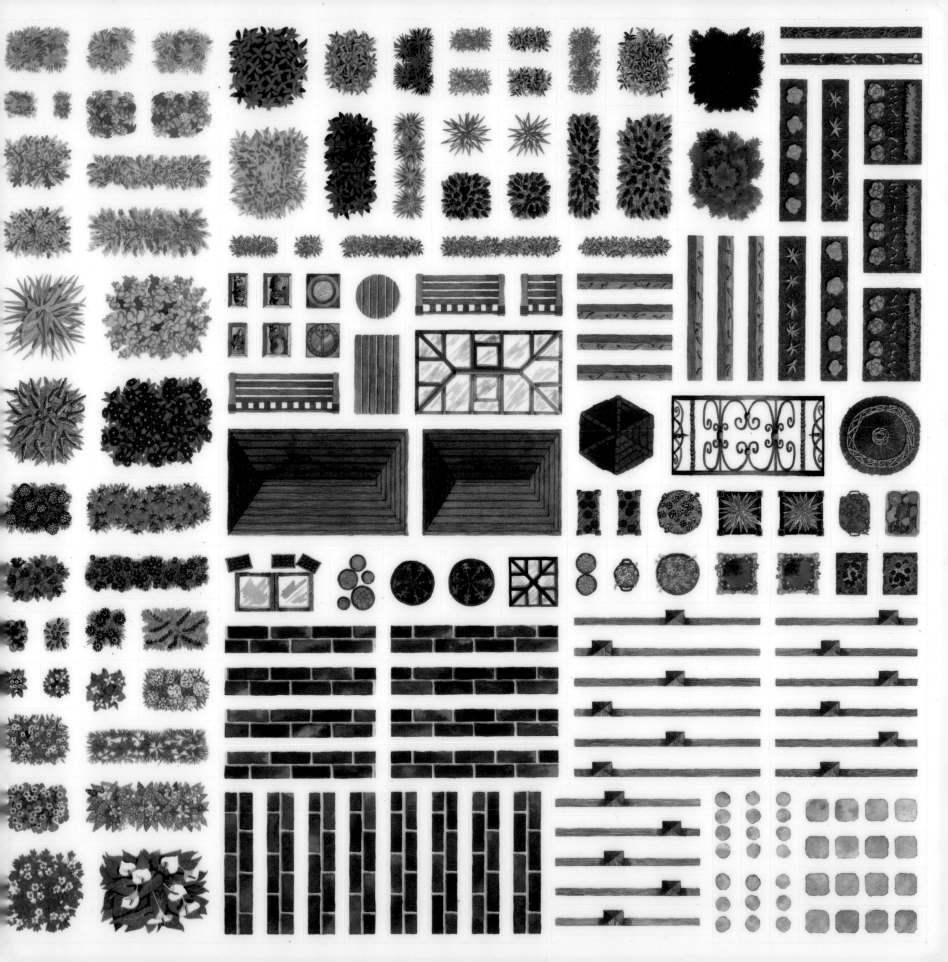